Investigating Knowledge Management

Professor Harry Scarbrough

Chris Carter

The Chartered Institute of Personnel and Development is the leading publisher of books and reports for personnel and training professionals, students, and all those concerned with the effective management and development of people at work. For full details of all our titles, please contact the Publishing Department:

Tel: 020 8263 3387
Fax: 020 8263 3850

E-mail: publish@cipd.co.uk

The catalogue of all CIPD titles can be viewed on the CIPD website:
www.cipd.co.uk/publications

Investigating Knowledge Management

Professor Harry Scarbrough
and Chris Carter
University of Leicester Management Centre

First published 2000

Cover design by Curve
Designed and typeset by Beacon GDT
Printed in Great Britain by Short Run Press

British Library Cataloguing in Publication Data
A catalogue record for this book is available from the British Library

ISBN 0 85292 899 8

Chartered Institute of Personnel and Development,
CIPD House, Camp Road, London SW19 4UX

Tel: 020 8971 9000
Fax: 020 8263 3333
Website: www.cipd.co.uk

Incorporated by Royal Charter. Registered charity no. 1079797.

Contents

Foreword

The knowledge economy is fast taking shape. Mobilising an organisation's knowledge resources in order to achieve organisational objectives is an increasingly critical issue for corporate strategists. Knowledge management has, however, become mainly a matter of optimising knowledge capture, flows and applications; the people development issues have figured, if at all, as hygiene factors. They have not been identified as key drivers of business performance in knowledge-based organisations.

The CIPD's Professional Policy Committee agreed in 1998 that the Institute should set up a major project to establish how personnel practitioners could be helped to make an impact on business performance through contributing to knowledge management. Since then *Knowledge Management: A literature review*, written for the Institute by Harry Scarbrough, Jacky Swan and John Preston, has confirmed the persistent domination of the knowledge management field by IT specialists, and the need to delineate the role of HR. This has been supplemented by the publication of *Case Studies in Knowledge Management* (edited by Harry Scarbrough and Jacky Swan) describing the effect of knowledge management strategies where the people issues have or have not been addressed.

The CIPD's Knowledge Management Project Steering Group, led by Trevor Bromelow, Personnel Director of Siemens (UK) Plc and the Institute's Vice-President, Training and Development, has more recently given the project a new focus to support HR professionals' practice, providing them with the understanding and tools to add value through knowledge management to their organisations. Not least we are looking at creating or strengthening ways in which the Institute itself, as a community of interest, can support members, including senior practitioners, to help themselves in developing their professionalism in the knowledge management area.

The role of people management and development specialists in mobilising an organisation's knowledge resources is the subject of well-established debate and research, but the current knowledge management debate raises important new questions about how HR impacts on business performance. This is why the CIPD has asked Harry Scarbrough and Chris Carter to survey for us the relevant research in knowledge management and its relationship to people management and development. We have also asked them to help us to 'know what we already know' by reviewing recent and current research commissioned by the CIPD and identifying what it tells us about HR and knowledge management. We have been keen to understand who is leading the thinking, what the major trends, debates and options are and what the key questions are on which further research needs to be targeted.

This report produced by Harry Scarbrough and Chris Carter makes for stimulating reading and should provide a significant resource for future researchers and enquiring practitioners. The report suggests five ways for personnel specialists to contribute to effective knowledge management and thereby to business performance: through models of best practice, motivating and retaining knowledge workers, linking knowledge management and HR management to business strategy, fostering social and human capital, and lastly, developing and sustaining learning within the organisation.

The hope is that this report will provide a starting point for translating existing research into effective HR practice that enables the HR professional to be recognised as an essential part of the mainstream corporate strategy team in knowledge-based organisations. The report also offers an agenda for further research that would make this an ongoing process. The CIPD will be considering how it can best contribute, through both research and supporting good practice, to strengthening the influence of HR managers and developers on knowledge creation and deployment in order to transform business performance.

Roy Harrison

Adviser, Training and Development
Chartered Institute of Personnel and Development

Executive summary

◘ This report presents the findings from a study of existing literature and research dealing with the interaction between human resource management (HRM) and knowledge management (KM) practices in organisations. The study aimed to establish what is known and what is being researched about the way HRM practices affect the management of knowledge in organisations. It used a range of research methods, including interviews with experts in the field, a survey of researchers and a review of the literature. It also examined the findings from existing CIPD-sponsored studies to identify possible implications for this issue.

◘ The review of CIPD-sponsored studies highlighted findings on the relationship between HRM practices and business performance. There was also relevant data on the problems of workplace learning. Studies also challenged the complacent view in some KM writing that organisations are harmonious environments in which individuals are happy to share knowledge with each other. In terms of implications for KM, these studies brought out a number of possible parallels between the effectiveness of HRM and KM. In particular, they implied a need to ensure the consistency of KM policies and to relate them to wider business strategy. A further set of CIPD studies is also reported. These have a great potential to illuminate the interaction with KM, but are still at an early stage of development.

◘ In addition to the review of CIPD-sponsored work, an e-mail survey identified a number of individuals and groups – mainly in the UK but also internationally – who are carrying out research in the KM area. Most of the researchers based their work within one of four major disciplines: information systems,

organisation studies, strategic management and human resource management. The survey of KM researchers found that a large percentage had identified HRM implications from the development of KM. However, while the survey indicated awareness of HRM issues, there was relatively little indication that HRM was a central component of the research that was being undertaken in the KM field. Only a relatively small percentage of the researchers could be classified as working within the HRM discipline.

◘ A review of the wider literature relevant to KM and HRM identified five major perspectives on the possible HRM contribution:

– Best practice perspective: here all organisations are seen to benefit directly from adopting best practice in HRM. The implication is that the best practice model will help to secure the appropriate co-operation and commitment to secure the success of KM.

– Knowledge work perspective: this focuses on the need to tailor HRM policies to the distinctive characteristics of knowledge-workers, especially their motivational needs in terms of work autonomy, careers, etc.

– Congruence perspective: based on recent work at Harvard Business School, this model suggests that HRM's effect will be enhanced by ensuring that HRM practices are matched with KM practices in the context of overall business strategy. Two major strategies are identified – codification and personalisation.

– Human and social capital perspective: this draws attention to the implications of HRM for the development of human and social resources within the organisation. These underpin the success of KM initiatives and are mobilised in the longer term as organisational capabilities.

– Learning perspective: this perspective encompasses two major strands, namely, organisational and community learning. The learning organisation is an influential model of the way in which knowledge and learning can be applied to organisational goals. It also relies heavily on HRM support. Meanwhile, the notion of 'communities of practice' draws attention to the way in which much tacit knowledge is created and shared within practitioner groups. This has implications in terms of the impact of HRM practices on different communities.

◘ This review and analysis is followed by a concluding chapter that draws on the research data to identify gaps and biases in existing studies. In particular, the chapter argues that optimistic signs of the emergence of a people-centred second- generation approach to KM need to be treated carefully. There is a danger that HRM factors such as culture and attitudes are being cited in a tokenistic fashion. HRM may be viewed as a hygiene factor to explain KM failure. To avoid this danger the chapter draws on the findings of the research to differentiate the impacts and timescales of HRM practices in relation to the management of knowledge. It identifies three major points of leverage, which are termed 'policy', 'resource' and 'context'.

◘ The policy area highlights the importance of the alignment of HRM *policies* with KM and business strategy. This is a short-term focus. A medium-term focus, however, is the way in which HRM practices help to create and sustain human *resources* within the organisation – for example, through selection and retention, and through mechanisms that translate individual expertise into an organisational resource. Finally, *context* addresses the enduring impact of HRM practices on the social and cultural environment in which knowledge is created and shared. This underscores the long-term development of human and social capital, and the evolution of organisational capabilities.

◘ Each of these areas defines specific research questions that have practical outcomes in relation to aiding the success of KM developments and matching the needs of KM with the influence of HRM.

1 | Introduction

◘ **This chapter highlights the need for greater understanding of the contribution that human resource management (HRM) policy and practice can make to the effectiveness of knowledge management (KM) programmes in organisations.**

◘ **The need for such understanding is reinforced by evidence on the important influence that behavioural and cultural factors exert on the success or failure of KM initiatives.**

◘ **Awareness of the influence of such factors is steadily increasing, particularly amongst practitioners dealing with the realities of KM projects.**

◘ **Awareness alone is not enough. If we are to manage the way people engage with knowledge in organisations, we need a much more sophisticated appraisal of the specific contributions of differing HRM practices.**

This report addresses the need for greater understanding of the implications of knowledge management (hereafter KM) for the theory, policy and practice of what will broadly be termed human resource management (HRM). KM is defined more specifically below, but the term is essentially used here to refer to concepts and activities relating to the management of knowledge in organisations. In a similar way the label of HRM is used to encompass the whole area of management activity that is specifically concerned with the management of people.

Aims

In order to develop greater understanding of the contribution of HRM to KM, this report has been prepared on behalf of the CIPD by Harry Scarbrough and Chris Carter. The aims of this study are basically fourfold:

1   To identify the contribution of existing CIPD-sponsored research to a better understanding of the relationship between HRM and KM.

2   To survey recent and ongoing research activity in the KM field – primarily in the UK, but also internationally – particularly insofar as it addresses HRM issues.

3   To review and analyse the existing literature which locates KM and knowledge-related issues in an HRM context.

4   To outline the key issues and gaps in research that are relevant to defining a broad research agenda for the HRM implications of the management of knowledge.

The importance of HRM in the management of knowledge

There is little need to rehearse in this report the great upsurge we have seen in the theory and practice of knowledge management. The reasons for this upsurge – both cosmetic and substantial – are well known and are amply attested to by economic statistics, management conferences and media coverage. This report, however, reflects a

> ' ... in our rush to 'manage' knowledge as a new-found
> economic asset, we may be losing sight of some of the
> ingredients that help to create and sustain its value.'

concern that in our rush to 'manage' knowledge as a new-found economic asset, we may be losing sight of some of the ingredients that help to create and sustain its value. An earlier report that surveyed the literature on KM (Scarbrough *et al*, 1999) concluded that much of the existing output on this topic took a narrow, technocratic approach to managing knowledge. Tools and systems were emphasised, and knowledge was viewed as an object or commodity that could be readily transferred, stored and exploited, almost without human intervention.

The consequences of that approach were sketched out in a subsequent report (Scarbrough and Swan, 1999), which compiled a series of case studies, each of them dealing with different aspects of the management of knowledge. A number of these cases showed that in practice KM initiatives which centred primarily on IT tools and systems typically failed in their objectives. It seemed that knowledge was too tied up with the relationships, attitudes and motivation of people within the organisation to be readily extracted, packaged and communicated through a system of information.

The findings from those cases have subsequently been confirmed by other commentators. There is a growing reaction to the idea that knowledge can be managed through systems, without attending to the people involved. The misuse, neglect or failure of many such systems is leading to demands for a second-generation approach to KM (Blackler, 2000) in which people would be a central rather than a peripheral element. These demands are being voiced most stridently by managers and employees who find that their KM systems, be they intranets, groupware or databases, are failing to deliver the much-trumpeted improvements in performance and innovation. The need for a people-centred

approach to KM is thus being driven by practice and not by abstract theoretical concerns.

The demand that KM initiatives should place people at their heart is beginning to be reflected not only in managerial opinion but also in research studies of the implementation of KM. These repeatedly stress the importance of people and behavioural factors to the success of KM. Factors such as organisation culture (Petrash, 1996), attitudes to knowledge-sharing (Rajan *et al*, 1998) and motivation (Ruggles, 1998) are regularly cited as important enablers or constraints on the effectiveness of the implementation of KM. The importance of human responses and attitudes to KM looks set to become almost a shibboleth of the field.

But, while this increased awareness of the importance of behavioural factors is welcome – especially since it is sometimes so painfully won – it is also becoming clear that awareness alone is not enough. If attitudes, motivations and relationships are so important to our ability to create and exploit knowledge, it follows that we need much greater understanding of the way in which these factors can be managed. If we cannot manage the ways in which people engage with knowledge, we have little chance of managing knowledge itself.

This issue is the one that drives the aims and content of this report. What understandings do we already have, and what do we need to develop that will help us better integrate the management of people into the management of knowledge? These questions lead us to survey both the existing literature relevant to these questions and the array of ongoing research projects – primarily in the UK but also internationally – that may provide some purchase on it. We are seeking to draw out the implications of a diverse range of studies for a better understanding of the specific processes and mechanisms through which the management of people – here we use 'HRM' as the preferred shorthand – influences or is affected by the development of KM. Is this influence quite local and specific; the unexpected consequence of reward systems, for instance? Or rather, is it broad and strategic, reflecting, say, the long-run development of trust through progressive employment policies? If managers can better understand these issues, they will be better equipped to pursue the exciting new opportunities opened up by KM, without the accompanying complement of Utopian goals or technological fixes. In our interrogation of what is already available and ongoing, we have tried to keep in mind these practical implications as an arbiter of the usefulness and relevance of what we have found.

Both the literature and the spread of research relating to KM are already enormous and are still growing. It follows that we need to qualify this ambitious aim with some methodological caveats. As we outline in the subsequent chapter, we cannot claim to have developed, within the timescale available, a fully realised and detailed assessment of all the different KM research activities that might be relevant to these questions. Also, we have had to be relatively parsimonious in our treatment of relevant aspects of KM. For example, we have not addressed the epistemological questions raised by this topic (these are debated, for instance, in Krogh and Roos, 1996). Nor have we been able within our time and space constraints to acknowledge the important work that is being carried out on the measurement and representation of intellectual capital, though this too has implications for HRM. Rather, we have sought to describe in as objective and accurate a fashion as possible what seem to us some of the major ideas, issues and activities that are relevant to advancing the debate on the people management aspects of KM. Our selection is necessarily partial and incomplete, but it reflects our wholehearted attempt to properly survey and represent this burgeoning field of work.

2 | Methodology

◪ **This chapter will describe the approach taken to data-gathering in this study. It involves a mixed methods approach, ie a combination of qualitative and quantitative methods, including an e-mail survey plus telephone interviews with particular groups and a literature review.**

◪ **The methodology is descriptive rather than analytic. The aim, as far as possible, is to let the researchers involved speak for themselves.**

◪ **The scope of the research is outlined – focusing on social science work (not technically oriented work such as knowledge engineering) that has the greatest relevance to HRM issues.**

Introduction

This chapter will outline the methodology underscoring the project. It begins by discussing the methodological assumptions employed here, and moves on to a detailed consideration of the techniques deployed in the operationalisation of the study. As a mapping exercise rather than a theoretical analysis, the study is intended to be non-judgmental and respectful to all actors and activities described here.

The relevant objectives of the report, as detailed in Chapter 1, can be briefly summarised as aiming to identify the key themes and nodes in the emerging field of KM, with the implications of and for HRM being of prime concern. This leads to a focus on KM research that has a social science orientation rather than the more technology-driven approaches that are still a significant element of this field. Also, our study concentrates largely on university-based research, with relatively little attention paid to other research sites, such as consultancies. This decision reflects the brevity of the timescale involved and the greater public accessibility of academic work. Finally, the study

concentrates on work explicitly concerned with the management of knowledge. It does not encompass work primarily dealing with more diffuse concepts such as knowledge work or organisational knowledge.

Our research strategy was iterative, but can be broadly characterised into six planned stages, which are outlined below.

Phase One: Internet search, conference analysis and library search

As the first stage in the mapping of the KM field, extensive searches were made of university websites, in order to determine locations where research was taking place. The analysis sought to identify: KM researchers; the content of their research; the existence of KM research grants; and publications in the field. The search of the websites extended to UK, Irish, North American and Australasian centres of research. In addition, contributions were analysed from two of the most recent conferences at which KM research has been presented: the Warwick University BPRC Conference on 'Knowledge Management:

Concepts and Controversies' (2000) and the University of Massachusetts 'Re-Organizing Knowledge' Conference (1999). A library search was also carried out to ascertain recent publications in KM.

Phase One obviously rests on the, not unreasonable, assumption that much research activity in this area is available on the Internet and through conferences. As such, phase one of the research programme aimed to provide a broad and indicative account of the KM field, helping to inform subsequent search activity.

Phase Two: E-mail questionnaire

The use of an e-mail questionnaire had several advantages. First, it enabled us in part to 'triangulate' the findings from phase one, ie establish whether the findings from phase one are reflected in primary data. Second, it allowed us to extend the analysis in phase one by eliciting the opinions of those working in the field of KM. Thus, the design of the questionnaire was in part a survey of KM activities, but it also posed qualitative questions, such as asking for comments on the field. In an attempt to increase the response rate, the questionnaire was designed to be completed by the respondent in 10 minutes. A further incentive, of offering an electronic summary of this report to all respondents, was also employed. Given researchers' extensive use of e-mail, its distribution via this medium enhanced speed of response and thereby the production of survey findings.

The questionnaire was sent to academics on two major distribution lists: one was the members of a mailbase on knowledge and organisations (know-org) and the other the list of participants at the recent BPRC conference on KM. Each of these lists contained over 200 names, providing, with some overlap, around 300–350 possible respondents. This sample also had the merit of being composed fairly exclusively of people with an active interest in the field of KM, of which the great majority would be expected to evince some kind of research interest. By the end of a four-week period (admittedly in the summer period when holidays would impact on response rates) 45 questionnaires were returned, a number of which incorporated responses from a research centre rather than individuals. This is a reasonable rate of response, particularly given the international coverage it provided, with replies from Europe, Australasia and the USA as well as the UK. Moreover, the vast majority of respondents were actively researching or publishing in the KM field.

The content of the questionnaire can be seen in Table 1.

It is necessary to discuss the rationale for each question. First, however, it should be noted that the questionnaire poses both strictly descriptive and more opinion-based questions.

Question 1 was intended quite simply to determine the disciplinary affiliations of researchers, reflecting the 'newness' of KM and its characteristic of drawing researchers from a variety of more established disciplines. The expectation here was that the discipline may impact on approaches, concerns and definitions of KM.

Questions 2, 4 and 5 were aimed at building up a picture of current sites of research on KM. Question 3 sought to make explicit the links between current research and key HRM issues. Questions 6 and 7 sought to elicit perceptions of leading thinkers and research centres. The final question was posed to ascertain the views of KM researchers on the way they saw the subject developing.

Table 1 | E-mail questionnaire

Knowledge Management Questionnaire

1. How would you describe the core discipline on which your knowledge management research is based?

  – Strategy

  – Information Systems

  – Accounting

  – Organisation Studies

  – Human Resource Management

  – International Management

  – Other ... please specify

2. Does your institution have a knowledge management research group?

  – If so please indicate the numbers of full-time equivalent staff involved

3. Please indicate whether your KM research has implications for HRM policy and practice in the following areas:

  (i) Recruitment and selection

  (ii) Training and development in the workplace

  (iii) Reward and appraisal systems

  (iv) Organisational and cultural change

  (v) Other HRM issues (please specify)

4. Do you currently have research funding to investigate knowledge management? Yes/No

  – If yes, what is the source of your research funds?

5. Have you published in the field of knowledge management? Yes/No

  – If yes, please give details.

6. Who, in your view, are currently the three leading researchers on knowledge management?

7. Which academic centres do you consider to be at the forefront of research into knowledge management?

8. What do you consider to be the key issues facing knowledge management as a subject area?

It is important to note that the questionnaire findings are used here primarily as a guide rather than as a means of making definitive statements about the field of KM. While we believe that the sample is significant, it would be mistaken to use it as the basis for making sweeping generalisations. Despite our efforts to make it otherwise, our study no doubt demonstrates an ethnocentric bias in that its prime focus is on the UK. This was probably inevitable in view of the timescale for the project combined with the time of year of the study.

Phase Three: Codification

The questionnaires were coded according to academic discipline. The data collected on HRM were used to identify any existing, explicit interfaces between the two disciplines. The final questions were analysed to determine particularly popular centres and academics.

Phase Four: Expert interviews

The raw data was further analysed through follow-up interviews with leading academics who were able to provide expert commentary on this developing field. The interviews were preceded by e-mails, and were conducted over the phone. The interviews were more detailed explorations of the areas covered by the questionnaire; they were unstructured, which allowed the interviewees to express freely their views on KM. The follow-up interviews were a means of generating more detailed and contextual data on the field of KM. They were also a means of getting recognised experts to comment on the field. Professors Baden-Fuller, Clark, Grant and Mueller all generously participated in informal interviews.

Phase Five: CIPD-commissioned research

Part of the terms of reference for this project entailed examining research, both past and present, commissioned by the CIPD. The objective was twofold: first, to determine whether the findings from extant research projects had a saliency for KM; secondly, to ascertain the potential crossover between ongoing projects and KM. One of the researchers visited the CIPD library, in Wimbledon, and analysed the recent CIPD reports (from 1995 to date). This work was followed by a summary of projects that had a particular purchase on KM. In terms of addressing the issue of ongoing projects, the researchers selected, from a list prepared by the CIPD, projects that appeared to have the greatest potential contribution to this report. Then, wherever possible, a member of each relevant research team was contacted, in order to discuss in detail the content of the project and potential overlaps with KM.

Phase Six: Reflexive monitoring

On completion of the first draft of the research findings, colleagues from the KM community in the UK were invited to comment on our interpretation of the field and its implications for HRM. These discussions were useful in terms of peer review and the validation of the final report for the CIPD.

3 | Review of CIPD-sponsored research

◘ **This chapter reviews recent and current research sponsored by the CIPD. It seeks to establish the contribution of existing work to the better understanding of the management of knowledge in organisations.**

◘ **Our study shows that CIPD-sponsored work to date helps to establish the importance of HRM involvement in the development of KM. HRM's influence on overall business performance underlines its potential contribution to the effective development of KM programmes.**

◘ **Lessons that can be learned from existing research on HRM include: the limitations of formal systems; the community-based nature of learning and tacit knowledge; and the relevance of different perspectives on the way management practices influence performance.**

This review is based on documentary analysis and interviews with some of the CIPD-sponsored researchers whose work is most relevant. The aim here will be to investigate existing and ongoing work into the field of HRM in order to identify potential linkages with KM issues. This will help to outline a research agenda for work on KM: what do HR practitioners really need to know about KM based on the existing CIPD studies in this area? The chapter will then shift its attention to ongoing research commissioned by the CIPD, examining the possible implications it might have for KM.

Background literature

As a major funding body for research addressing HRM, the CIPD has in recent years commissioned and published, through its Issues in People Management series, a substantial body of research. While the research, excepting Scarbrough and Swan (1999), was not concerned with KM *per se*, it is nonetheless useful to revisit this literature in order to identify findings that may have a particular resonance for the theory and

practice of KM. In the concise section that follows, the major findings and suggestions of the research projects will be outlined.

The Impact of People Management Practices on Business Performance: A literature review, 1999 (Ray Richardson and Marc Thompson)

This study sought to review the extant studies exploring the relationship between HRM and business performance. The backdrop to this study was the plethora, 30 or more, of research studies that had made claims *vis-a-vis* the causality between HRM and bottom-line financial performance. In outlining the terrain, the authors drew attention to the three major perspectives on the way in which HR practices could be held to impact upon business performance. First, there was the model of 'best practice', a notion that basically asserts there are superior practices that should be adopted by all organisations. Such a view in essence transcends issues of cultural, institutional and societal context. The second perspective was that of contingency theory, which seeks a fit between the organisational strategy and its HRM function. The third perspective focused on the impact of so-called 'bundles' of practices, ie, to quote the authors (1999, p xi): 'specific combinations of HR practices can be identified which generate higher business performance, but these combinations will vary by organisational context'.

Overall, the study concluded of these different perspectives that a healthy scepticism should be brought to bear on claims of a 'universal best practice HR strategy', something that the authors viewed as being 'premature' (p30), noting that 'it is unlikely that merely adopting a specified set of HR policies is the high road to success' (p30). Instead they adopted a pragmatic stance towards best practice, arguing that: 'Managers should not en masse be discarding their present arrangements. That is not to say that the studies on which such claims are based are without interest. Quite the contrary, and they give a checklist of policy combinations which organisations should very actively consider adopting' (p30).

Implications for KM

This study makes a useful contribution to current debate by developing an analytical approach to the relationship between HRM practices and business performance. As the authors observe, the links between practice and performance are complex, and our view of them will be profoundly influenced by the implicit perspective we adopt. The need to be conscious of different causal models of business performance is obviously highly relevant to the analysis of the effectiveness of KM. In the existing KM literature, however, it is typically glossed over by the benign assumption that knowledge per se has a positive impact on performance, and, worse, that increasing the

supply of 'knowledge' will automatically enhance performance. These are both assumptions that are highly open to question, as subsequent chapters will demonstrate.

The Impact of People Management Practices on Business Performance, 1997 (Malcolm Patterson, Michael West, Rebecca Lawthom and Stephen Nickell)

This study was a review of various literatures that sought to make links between people management practices and performance. In contrast to the scepticism of the previous report, this review reached a more positive conclusion, namely, that 'these results very clearly indicate the importance of people management practices in predicting company performance' (p xi). In disaggregating this proposition, the review explored four problematics: the role of job satisfaction in relation to performance; the role of organisational culture; the relationship between human resource practices, profit and productivity; and a determination of which management practices were most important in predicting company performance. On the basis of their investigations, the authors confidently arrived at a number of conclusions on these different points, asserting that:

- ◘ 'The more satisfied workers are with their jobs the better the company is likely to perform' (p x)

- ◘ 'cultural factors accounted for 10% of the variation in profitability between companies ... with concern for employee welfare being the most important. 29% of the variation of productivity over a three or four year period (can be explained) in human relations terms' (p x)

'HRM is likely to prove to be an important influence on the much-vaunted ability of KM to deliver improved levels of innovation and efficiency.'

◘ 'HRM practices taken together explain 19% of the variation between companies in change in profitability' (p x)

◘ 'HRM practices are more powerful predictors of change in company performance than strategy, quality, technology or R&D' (p xi).

Implications for KM

The review by Patterson *et al* emphasises the importance of HRM, broadly defined, to organisational performance. It is not difficult to infer from this that HRM is likely to prove to be an important influence on the much-vaunted ability of KM to deliver improved levels of innovation and efficiency. Equally important is the way the review demonstrates the centrality of HRM practices to achieving business performance, both in terms of steady-state improvements and in terms of change and turnarounds in performance. Translating this to the context of KM implementation, it suggests that to be wholly realised the organisational and technological changes associated with KM depend on the enabling effect of HRM changes.

Workplace Learning, Culture and Performance, 1999 (Eliot Stern and Elizabeth Sommerlad)

This study was an attempt to discuss and synthesise the issues of learning in the workplace, the way they relate to the culture of the organisation and the impact, if any, they may have on business performance. Its concerns reflected the growth of interest in the 'learning organisation' during the 1990s. Stern and Sommerlad's work is wide-ranging and reached some interesting conclusions about the realities of workplace learning, as outlined below:

◘ 'We do not have a good picture of how much workplace learning activity is actually going on, or what form it takes … Because informal training and learning is so intrinsically linked to the day-to-day operation of the company, it virtually defies quantitative measurement' (p xi)

◘ 'The workplace learning practices of companies often lag behind a commitment to the philosophy of a "learning organisation", even among those companies reputed to be "leading edge" in their human resource development strategies' (p xii)

◘ 'Those responsible for introducing new forms of working or learning often have insufficient regard for the micro-politics of the workplace' (p xii)

◘ 'certain methodologies, such as on-the-job training or the "key worker"/Meister concept are highly contextualised. They work well where they have a close fit with underlying values and institutional frameworks. Their embedded nature is such that transfer to a setting calls for a sophisticated adaptation process' (p xiv).

Implications for KM

This study has some specific contributions to make to our discussion. These include, in particular, the findings about the limitations of formal policy and systems, and the influence of context on a firm's ability to transfer new methods and ideas. These points – which are amply supported by other studies of organisations – are highly pertinent to KM programmes. Managers would be well advised to bear them in mind in implementing such programmes. Also, the study highlights the way that workplace learning is embedded in the micro-politics and practices of organisations. This is a cautionary reminder that tacit knowledge is more elusive than current debate tends to suggest. Certainly, it underlines the relative effectiveness of the informal interactions of 'communities of practice' in sharing knowledge, compared to the more limited reach of formal systems.

Overall, then, Stern and Sommerlad's study can be viewed as a good guide to the potential problems and pitfalls faced by KM. Thus, a boardroom commitment to KM may bear little relation to the actual implementation of an initiative. Moreover, in light of these findings, the call for KM to share and codify knowledge must be regarded as an inherently political act and managed as such. It cannot be viewed as a neutral, technical intervention because it may have profound implications for the distribution of power in organisations. The sovereign cliché 'knowledge is power' is used so glibly that managers sometimes forget that it has real, practical consequences – consequences that can easily derail KM initiatives that lack such political sensitivity. Finally, this study should lead us to question the universal applicability of KM concepts and tools. Not only is knowledge more or less biddable depending on context, but firms' ability to adopt these new ideas will inevitably involve more than a little local difficulty and adaptation.

Employment Relations, HRM and Business Performance, 2000 (David Guest, Jonathan Michie, Maura Sheehan and Neil Conway)

This analysis of the 1998 WERS study sought to look specifically at the relationships between employment relations, HRM and their possible impacts on business performance. The findings were mixed. In the private sector, for example, the analysis found a 'clear link between the use of more human resource practices and greater employee involvement, and positive employee satisfaction and commitment, higher productivity and better financial performance' (p xii). This confirmed a strong association between human resource management and employee attitudes and workplace performance in the private sector (p51). However, later the authors noted that this was not a 'straightforward link' and 'we cannot assert with confidence that it is a causal link' (p52). Also, they failed to find 'any bundles of human resource practices' from their analysis. They comment that: 'practices were rather general and did not fall into a coherent set of what have been variously described as high commitment or high performance practices'. Such practices in any case were not widespread in the private sector. This rather dispiriting conclusion from the HR professional's point of view was, however, partially mitigated by the finding that the role of the personnel department was the most important determinant of the number of (HR) practices adopted. More worryingly, though, the latter had no association with human resource strategy – a finding that was even further exacerbated in the public sector, where 'human resource practices have virtually no association with outcomes' (p52).

This account of the organisational impact of HRM practices – good in some areas, patchy in others, and apparently non-existent in the public sector – provides food for thought as far as HRM practitioners are concerned. It is, however, more positive on some behavioural issues, where it is suggested that employees 'display moderate levels of satisfaction and commitment', and that managers 'report considerable growth in the importance of employee involvement'.

The report concludes with one positive finding, namely, that where it is possible to build high trust then positive pay-offs for all partners can result. But it also expresses a call for more work to be done: 'We need to learn more about good practices and new practices, we remain very ignorant about the "black holes". Why do managers persist in the use of sub-optimal practices? What are their values and how far are they aware of alternative approaches?' Substantively, it says: 'We need more evidence from cases about the achievement of change in organisations that have gone from black holes to shining stars in the firmament of employee relations and HRM' (p54).

Implications for KM

Guest *et al*'s study has a number of important implications for KM. The first is in the distinction between the public and the private sectors. The findings suggest the difficulties of making any links between HR practices and performance in the case of public sector organisations. In a comment that could equally apply to KM initiatives, the authors note the disruptive impact of centralised state pressure on managers' ability to sustain a coherent approach to new practices and programmes. In relation to the private sector, it would seem that Guest *et al*'s findings have some purchase on KM. On the one hand, HRM practices delivering high trust and high commitment would seem to be very important in enabling KM. On the other hand, the limited take-up of these practices would caution against the view that employees will automatically welcome KM initiatives with great enthusiasm. Equally a cause for concern is the perceived lack of influence that HR departments exert upon HR strategy. This would tend to refute the argument – which we outline in Chapter 5 – that management practices, including HRM and KM, can be smoothly harmonised and integrated with overall business strategy.

How Dissatisfied are British Workers? A survey of surveys, 1999 (David Guest and Neil Conway)

This 'survey of surveys' was commissioned by the CIPD to provide an overview of the numerous pieces of extant work that sought to investigate dissatisfaction and insecurity in the workplace. Mindful of the objectives of KM, and that in part it relies on the willingness of employees to share their knowledge, quantitative studies into the nature of dissatisfaction may well be illuminating in terms of how realistic the aims of KM are in the context of the British workplace. Some writers (see Prichard *et al*, 2000) have criticised writing on KM for its cosy unitary assumptions about working in organisations. This survey sheds some light on levels of satisfaction in the British workplace. In part, Guest and Conway sought to explain what they took to be a 'gap between the rhetoric of a dissatisfied workforce and the reality of a much more positive overall picture' (p30). They argued that: 'The majority of British workers are satisfied, committed to their employing organisation and feel secure in their employment' (p30). But, they noted: 'There is a sizeable minority of dissatisfied and insecure workers. They are most likely to be traditional, male blue collar workers who are trade union members' (p31).

Importantly, Guest and Conway find a close relationship between satisfaction levels and HRM practices: 'Dissatisfaction is also closely linked to aspects of organisational policy and practice. Satisfaction, commitment, feelings of job security and good employment relations are likely to be higher in those places where positive HR practices are in place and where there is a climate of involvement and partnership. These policies and practices account for a significant proportion of the variation in job satisfaction' (p31). They, therefore, reach the positive conclusion that: 'If progressive HR practices are in place and there is a climate of partnership and involvement, then levels of satisfaction and commitment, along with feelings of job security and positive employer–employee relations are likely to be much higher' (p29).

Implications for KM

These findings might reflect what many feel intuitively, namely, that satisfaction in the workplace is linked to factors such as the policy and practice of an organisation. What is of greater relevance here is the further confirmation the study provides of a link between progressive HRM practices and satisfaction in the workplace. This suggests that specific HRM practices have specific behavioural effects – an important finding given the reliance of KM programmes on behavioural attributes such as trust, organisational identification and positive attitudes towards the sharing of knowledge. Moreover, the study also indicates the long-term nature of some of these effects, which produce satisfaction but also condition the climate and culture of the organisation. These long-term effects are important ingredients in the development of human and social capital, as we shall discuss in later chapters.

Effective People Management: Initial findings of the Future of Work study, 2000 (David Guest, Jonathan Michie, Maura Sheehan, Neil Conway and Melvina Metochi)

This report describes the findings from research that has been part-funded by both the ESRC and the CIPD. This involved telephone interviews with HRM managers and chief executives from a total of 835 organisations – probably the largest

company-level survey of its kind undertaken in the UK.

The aim of the study was to explore the impact of HRM practices on business performance through a model that examined links between business strategy, HRM practices, employee attitudes and behaviour, and measures of performance. In particular, the distinctive contribution of this study was that it sought to establish not only whether HRM practices affected performance but *how* that effect was achieved.

In addressing these issues, however, the study also highlighted the relatively low adoption of HR practices in UK organisations. It found, for instance, that only 1 per cent of the companies surveyed had adopted more than three-quarters of a key list of typical HR practices. Also, the report claimed that 'most managers only pay lip service to the idea that people are their most important assets' – only 10 per cent of those surveyed made people issues a top priority ahead of financial and marketing issues.

Against this backdrop, the analysis of interview data helped to unpack the complex relationships between HRM practices and performance. Through its cross-sectional data, the analysis was able to establish an association – if not a causal relationship – between, respectively, the effectiveness of HRM practices, employee attitudes and behaviour, and both internal and external performance indicators. The key finding here was the importance of the *effectiveness* of HRM practices – in other words, what counted in performance terms was not simply the existence of such practices but how well they were implemented.

The report comes to the important conclusion that 'the effective use of a wide range of progressive HR practices is linked to superior performance' (px) and that employee attitudes and behaviour are a crucial element of that link. Equally important, the report underscores the 'key role for HRM and for a focus on employees for successful economic performance' (p38). These findings are only one outcome from a longer-term research programme and are hedged around by various caveats. In particular, the study found a worrying, but possibly significant, lack of consensus between chief executives and HRM managers on the effectiveness of HRM practices. On the other hand, by opening up the 'black box' of the relationship between HRM and business performance, and by highlighting the critical role of HRM effectiveness, the study helps to advance the HRM research agenda into new and important areas.

Implications for KM

In certain respects, this study reinforces previous CIPD-sponsored studies by emphasising the impact of HRM practices on business performance. However, this study makes two distinctive contributions that are especially relevant to the debate on KM. First, its focus on the relative effectiveness of HRM practices as a crucial factor can be readily extended to discussion of KM practices. The implication is that we should be less concerned with the formal adoption of KM practices – for example, key learnings databases or corporate yellow pages – than with the way they are applied and used in practice. This concern with effectiveness is a cautionary reminder that the gap between rhetoric and reality, which is certainly a feature of HRM practice, can equally apply to other management practices too. Thus new KM tools and techniques have no value unless they are fully assimilated into the way people work.

A second contribution from this study is its identification of employee attitudes and behaviour as an important mediating influence on business performance. In other words, HRM practices influence business performance *through* their implications for employee attitudes and behaviour. This influence, which is obviously related to the effectiveness variable noted above, highlights the need to take employee responses into account when evaluating the competitive effect of management practices. Again, this point is clearly paralleled in the debate on KM. Many KM initiatives seem to assume that there is a direct relationship between the technological capability to manage knowledge and the competitive position of the organisation. A greater recognition of the mediating role of employee behaviour would help to correct this kind of wishful thinking.

Research in progress

People Management and Performance
(University of Bath, School of Management; Professor John Purcell; timescale January 2000 – July 2002)

Research here centres on identifying the relationships between HR policy and practice and performance outcomes. It is aimed at countering and/or complementing some recent studies that have addressed these relationships through survey-based analyses.

The research involves in-depth case studies of specified business units within 12 companies. This allows data to be gathered on performance indicators and HRM policies and practices within each unit. The project aims to encompass all the key variables mediating the relationship between HRM and performance through interviews that elicit the perceptions and attitudes of a range of personnel. The research will generate recommendations on HRM practice, but will link these to contextual factors.

Interview questions will be informed by consideration of social and intellectual capital. The research will investigate a range of knowledge-related issues, including networking, communications and learning. Three of the firms are knowledge-based, but other firms are also increasingly concerned with exploitation of knowledge by front-line employees. The findings are likely to encompass some KM issues, particularly in terms of their mediating effect on employee work and business performance.

People and Performance in Growing Knowledge-Intensive Firms (timescale September 2000 – July 2002)

This project is a further development of the major study outlined above. It has a specific focus on small and medium-sized knowledge-intensive firms, drawn from the computer and media services sector (ie IT consultancy, software, publishing and new media). This project will develop a sharper focus on knowledge-related issues, in particular the economics of training and development and the role of formalised learning.

Organisational Change and the Psychological Contract (King's College, University of London; Professor David Guest, Neil Conway and Adrian Patch; December 2000)

This project sought to determine the impact that different types of change (redundancy, culture change, the implementation of new technology, etc.) had upon the psychological contract, especially in terms of whether employees felt that the organisation had kept its promises. The findings from the study suggest that different

types of change seemed to have different impacts on the psychological contract. For instance, redundancy programmes were generally viewed as having a negative impact on job satisfaction and the like. In contrast, the implementation of new technology had the opposite effect. Interestingly, initiatives such as cultural change programmes had a neutral impact on the psychological contract.

The Psychological Contract in the Public Sector (October 2000)

This study builds on existing work by Guest and Conway that suggests there are key differences in respect of the impact of HRM practices on performance between the public and private sectors. This study seeks to explore the differences in more detail by exploring public/private distinctions in relation to the psychological contract. The study goes further by disaggregating the public sector into key groups, such as central government workers, local government workers, etc. This approach indicates that in addition to the general differences between the public/private sector, there are also important distinctions within the public sector.

Employers and the Psychological Contract (2001)

This study is at the data analysis stage, and it is seeking to contribute to understandings of how employers conceive of and make attempts to use the psychological contract.

Overall, the impact of these three studies will be to provide firm empirical evidence that will help both HRM professionals and academics alike understand the psychological contract in more detail. These studies were not designed to examine specifically the implications for KM, and it would be somewhat problematic to make blanket

'The unifying theme in these studies is the notion that good HRM policies translate into bottom-line business performance. Yet what is clear is that this is far from a straightforward or linear relationship.'

generalisations on the practice of KM from them. Notwithstanding such reservations, there are of course important insights that can be gleaned from work into the psychological contract and how this might impact on the willingness or capacity of employees to participate in KM programmes.

Knowledge Work and Intellectual Capital

While not commissioned by the CIPD, Professor Guest and Adrian Patch are currently undertaking a parallel project that is of direct significance to the interests of HRM and KM. This is an investigation of the employment relationship in terms of exploring issues surrounding the ownership of intellectual capital and the utilisation of human and social capital. Put simply, the question being asked is: 'what happens when knowledge workers leave the organisation?' Such a question goes to the very heart of the dilemma faced by many contemporary organisations, for if knowledge workers are 'key knowledge agents' within an organisation, then their departure, especially to competitors, may have far-reaching implications. This study will look particularly at the way in which colleagues deal with the departure of a knowledge worker from an organisation. Deploying 360-degree research techniques, whereby managers, senior managers and staff are all interviewed on the same subject, the study investigates the problems of accessing knowledge and of the way in which people take responsibility for KM practices. This research explores important issues surrounding knowledge work, which include the potential tensions between the interests of organisations and knowledge workers, especially with regard to issues of the ownership, exploitation and control of knowledge.

The field work is currently being negotiated but it will be taking place in the IT, telecommunications, pharmaceuticals and finance sectors, all of which are characterised as being populated by knowledge workers. This project has potentially profound implications for the study of KM. It engages with central problems of KM, ie in terms of the loss of expertise and in the tensions of attempting to access knowledge in environments where there are inevitable tensions in the employment relationship. The policy implications of this work lie in their capacity to provide guidance on the way such tensions might be dissipated.

Management of Knowledge and Knowledge Workers (Glasgow University; Professors Phillip Beaumont and Laurie Hunter; timescale October 2000 – October 2001)

This research will focus on what knowledge management means for HR professionals and how they can help their organisations manage knowledge and knowledge workers effectively. The work will include exploration of the notions of trust and the psychological contract and, in particular, sources of identity and motivation for knowledge workers.

Conclusions

This chapter has engaged with recent research commissioned by the CIPD. The specific aim has been to deconstruct the chief findings of the studies in order to determine whether they have any purchase on the current debate. While not dealing with KM *per se*, each of the studies profiled raise important points that deserve serious consideration from both KM theorists and practitioners alike.

The unifying theme in these studies is the notion that good HRM policies translate into bottom-line business performance. Yet what is clear is that this is far from a straightforward or linear relationship. The mediating links between HRM and business performance remain ambiguous. This lack of clarity, however, does not detract from the importance HRM undoubtedly has in the workplace. The CIPD-commissioned studies are illustrative of the wide range of effects wrought by HRM in the workplace. For instance, the studies by Patterson *et al* (1997) and Richardson and Thompson (1999) are useful reminders of the positive impact HRM can have on business performance. Likewise, recent work by Guest *et al* (2000) attests to the importance, at least in the private sector, of HRM practices as a means of delivering organisational benefits. More specifically, while adopting a pragmatic, cautious approach to HRM, it could also be seen that issues such as job satisfaction can feed through into bottom-line performance.

At the level of programmatic change, the study by Stern and Sommerlad (1999) raises important points in regard to the reception of new initiatives in the workplace. They emphasise that practice often lags behind commitment to an initiative. They also recognise that workplaces are highly politicised and as such may prove to be hostile environments for HRM initiatives. Following on from this point, for them an HRM initiative needs to be sensitive to a specific organisational context.

The gap between rhetoric and reality noted by Stern and Sommerlad finds an echo too in the 'Effective People Management' study by Guest *et al*. The finding that the effectiveness of HRM practices – the 'how' as much as the 'what' – is so important in shaping business performance

underlines the importance of the micro-politics of practical management action. In particular, this study demonstrates that employee attitudes and behaviour are an important mediating influence on business performance. It suggests that the need for employee commitment is more than a platitude but has real purchase on the way organisations compete in the current business environment.

In short, the studies published in the Issues of People Management series are important in and of themselves. And, looking to the future, the ongoing studies being led by Professors Purcell and Guest respectively will be of direct interest both for academics and practitioners who are interested in KM but who recognise the centrality of an HRM philosophy to successful organisational practices.

In terms of their specific implications for KM, three major issues emerge from these studies, which will be the subject of further analysis in subsequent chapters. First, the consistent finding that HRM practices influence business performance by mediating behavioural responses in the organisation. This mediating effect of HRM practice represents an important means of supporting and sustaining KM initiatives. Second, there is the analysis of different models of the relationship between HRM and business performance. This is directly relevant to the study of the effects of KM, as we discuss in Chapter 5. Finally, we note the importance of registering the timescales over which HRM practices can influence behaviour, including long-term effects through the shaping of climate and culture. This again will be an important point for future discussion, especially in the concluding chapter.

4 | Surveying the field of knowledge management

◘ **This chapter reviews current research on KM and seeks to highlight those studies that address implications for HRM. It identifies relevant research through descriptions of programmes, centres and leading thinkers.**

◘ **Social science research on KM is currently being conducted from four major disciplinary perspectives: organisation studies, strategic management, information systems and HRM.**

◘ **The majority of social science researchers recognise HRM implications from their work, particularly in relation to training and development and organisational and cultural change.**

Introduction

This chapter presents the results of research carried out into the major themes and nodes that characterise current KM research. At this point, it is important to reiterate the caveat outlined in the methodology, namely, that this chapter should not be regarded as a definitive *omnium gatherum* of KM research. Rather it should be read as a 'snapshot' of a dynamic field. Given the timescale within which this research was conducted and the extent of research related to KM, this report cannot claim to offer a detailed picture of all current work. Inevitably, some groups or individuals may feel their work has been overlooked or under-represented. Within the study's constraints, however, we have sought to produce an account that is a reasonable reflection of the richness and diversity of this field, if not of every individual project currently being undertaken within it. We have also sought to provide contact points and resources for readers seeking additional information in particular areas.

Research on KM is being conducted in a diverse range of contexts. Setting aside the specialised research that relates simply to KM technologies,

and which is outside the brief of this report, two major groupings are currently engaged in relevant work. The first group of researchers are those working in universities and business schools. Their work is the major focus of this chapter. The second group are working in private sector organisations, and particularly consultancy firms. All of the major consultancies have developing offerings in the KM area, and many are sponsoring practitioner-oriented studies to support their offerings. As the spread and innovativeness of KM practice has generally outstripped academic research by a comfortable margin, it is reasonable to suspect that much interesting work is being carried out in these private sector settings. Indeed, research on KM arguably reflects what has been called a new 'mode of knowledge production' in which knowledge is produced outside the ivory towers of the universities, directly in the context of use (Gibbons *et al*, 1994; Lyotard, 1984). Significantly, some of the leading thinkers on KM – for example, Laurence Prusak (Prusak, 1997) in the USA and David Snowden in the UK – are members of consultancy organisations. That being said, however, while some of the intellectual output from consultancies reaches the public arena – and is therefore reflected here – much of it remains proprietary and therefore falls outside the scope of the present report. Some indication of this proprietary knowledge can be gleaned from details of the consultancy websites, which we have incorporated in the Appendix on Internet resources.

The constitution of the KM field

One of the first points to note about the academic research being conducted on KM is that it is still heavily structured by specialist disciplines. In particular, as outlined in Figure 1, four major disciplines predominate as far as the human dimension of KM is concerned: strategic management, information systems, organisation studies and HRM itself. Researchers continue to work either exclusively within or at least predominantly from these longer-established discourses. Although KM represents a rich field for interdisciplinary work, the pressures towards specialisation in research tend to militate against working across boundaries. This situation might be viewed as ironic given that one of the major aims of KM practice is making knowledge available

across boundaries. But, more seriously, as we describe later, it also helps to explain the problems of developing a holistic picture that addresses both the people and technology elements of the equation.

Given this disciplinary tendency in existing research, the data presented in this chapter will be explored primarily from the perspective of different disciplines. The analytical usefulness of this approach is that it will serve to highlight the relative degree of fragmentation or fragile unity within the field of KM research. The chapter is therefore organised as follows. It begins with the presentation of the questionnaire results, followed by a commentary on the current research centres for KM. The main focus of this review is on the UK, although every attempt is made to highlight key research centres at business schools throughout the world. This will then be followed by a brief synthesis of the work of researchers identified as being leading figures in the field of KM.

Figure 1 | The making of KM

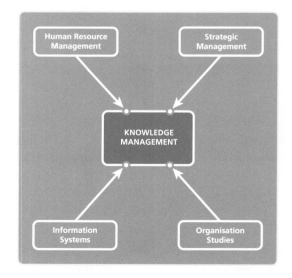

'KM not only elevates the theoretical scope of IS academics to the commanding heights of strategy and competitive advantage, it also affords a wide-ranging justification for investments in new IT systems.'

Questionnaire findings

This section will outline the findings from the questionnaire, sent out over e-mail during July 2000. Mindful of our view, as seen in Figure 1, that KM as an academic discourse has in effect been largely created by the contributions of academics from the disparate areas of information systems, strategy, organisation studies and human resource management, the questionnaire findings will be presented according to the four subject areas plus an additional category of 'interdisciplinary', where researchers have identified themselves as cutting across disciplines, either individually or collectively as part of a research group. This will then be followed by an aggregation of the research findings, bringing together all of the responses transcending the specific discipline.[1]

In terms of the breakdown of responses:

- 27% of respondents were 'interdisciplinary'

- 18% of respondents were from strategic management

- 23% of respondents were from organisation studies

- 14% of respondents were from HRM

- 18% of respondents were from information systems.

Information systems

Throughout its history the concerns of the discipline of information systems have been twofold: first, to explore the technical dimensions of computing; second, to engage at a more sociological or philosophical level with the social implications of technology (Bijker, 1993). Like the discipline of HRM, the development of information systems (IS) research has closely paralleled the role and responsibilities of IS practitioners. In particular, the discipline has tended to reflect the shifting importance and impact of IT in organisations. IS functions in organisations have evolved away from narrowly technical computing tasks towards distributed applications and eventually to more strategic and organisational concerns (Friedman and Cornford, 1989). At the same time, the academic discipline of IS has evolved away from the technical specialism of computing – very often emerging not within the computing departments of universities but within business schools. The scope of IS research also reflects this evolution, with its focus expressing the growing needs of IS practitioners for concepts that would address their growing role within organisations and at the same time legitimise it.

The IS interest in KM can be seen as a further iteration of this pattern. KM not only elevates the theoretical scope of IS academics to the commanding heights of strategy and competitive advantage, it also affords a wide-ranging justification for investments in new IT systems. To the extent that information flows can facilitate knowledge creation and exploitation, KM opens up new theoretical and practical possibilities for the IS contribution to organisations. For IS academics this raises important questions about the relationships between data, information and knowledge. And for IS functions it mandates a critical strategic role and defends it against attempts to turn IS expertise into a commodity through outsourcing contracts.

---

1. A number of the respondents to our e-mail survey cited Scarbrough and Swan in their listing of leading researchers. These responses have been disregarded on the grounds of a possible recency effect – the e-mail survey having been distributed by Scarbrough.

The information systems responses to the questionnaire amounted to 18 per cent of the sample. It is worth bearing in mind that this study was confined to responses from IS researchers who acknowledged an HRM dimension to their work. Without such a proviso, it would be expected that IS researchers would have been a much greater percentage of respondents than is the case.

Survey findings

☐ 75% of IS respondents reported that their institution possessed a KM research centre.

☐ Implications for HRM policy and practice:

– 25% of the sample claimed that their research had implications for recruitment and selection policy and practice

– 75% of the sample claimed that their research had implications for training and development in the workplace

– 25% of the sample claimed that their KM research had implications for reward and appraisal systems

– 75% of the sample claimed that their KM research had implications for organisational and cultural change policy and practice.

☐ 75% of the sample possessed research funds to investigate KM. Funding sources included the British ESRC, the European Union and the Swedish Government.

☐ 100% of the sample had published articles/ book chapters in the field of KM.

Major concerns facing the emerging subject area

A general view here was the importance of recognising human and behavioural factors. Thus 50 per cent contended that KM needed to engage further with the interaction between people and technology. One researcher described the challenge as follows: 'In general terms, what are the driving forces for the era of knowledge management: the role of culture, management, technology etc. … (more) specifically, how do we study the interaction between people and technology in KM settings?' Other issues included a greater concern with the relationship between KM and communities of practice.

At a more abstract level, there was a concern that the key challenge for KM was to reconcile the contradictions of KM. One researcher stated the contradictions as being: 'reconciling the central, unmanageable aspects of knowledge such as creativity, tacit dimensions, etc. with the desire to manage, and designing technologies that recognise the above'.

The key researchers identified by the IS respondents to the questionnaire were Claudio Ciborra and John Seely Brown.

Organisation studies

In recent years growing attention has been paid to KM from within the loosely based subject area of organisation studies. In a sense this is a reanimation of long-standing interests in issues of knowledge embedded in organisations (cf Burns and Stalker, 1961), through to more detailed studies of the capabilities – or the 'repertoire' – of an organisation (Whipp and Clark, 1986; Clark and Starkey, 1988; Smith *et al*, 1990). There has been a long-continuing research agenda within OS to prise open the 'black box' of knowledge in organisations. This has been a central theme of studies into innovation during the 1980s and 1990s (Clark and Staunton, 1989; Fincham *et al*, 1994). In addition, the 1990s witnessed numerous attempts by OS scholars to engage with programmed change initiatives (Wilson, 1992); examples include movements such as TQM (cf Wilkinson and Willmott, 1995) and BPR (Knights and Willmott, 2000). The emergence of KM as such, through the writings of authors such as Nonaka and Takeuchi (1995), combined with the production and promotion of KM programmes by the major management consultancies, and evidence of its widespread diffusion, make it an area of considerable interest to the OS community.

Survey findings

- 75% of OS respondents reported that their institution possessed a KM research centre. The number of full-time staff ranged between two and six members.

- 25% of respondents reported that they belonged to a research network, consisting of themselves and colleagues from other institutions.

- Implications for HRM policy and practice:

    - 20% of the sample claimed that their research had implications for recruitment and selection policy and practice.

    - 40% of the sample claimed that their research had implications for training and development in the workplace.

    - 0% of the sample claimed that their KM research had implications for reward and appraisal systems.

    - 80% of the sample claimed that their KM research had implications for organisational and cultural change policy and practice.

- 20% of the sample possessed research funds to investigate KM. Funding sources included the British EPSRC and the Swedish Government.

- 60% of the sample had published in the field of KM.

Major concerns facing the emerging subject area

The leading writers nominated here were Nonaka, Spender and Van Krogh. But organisation studies academics were as a cohort less willing to identify key researchers or major research centres. Only 50 per cent named researchers, with fewer naming particular centres. There was less reticence, however, in terms of talking about the challenges that lay ahead for KM. In a sense many of the concerns reflect those raised by Frank Blackler in a recent *People Management* article (22 June 2000). Blackler's point is first to relativise knowledge, ie to argue that there are no absolutes that transcend time and space. His second point is to suggest that the field is moving into a 'second generation', whereby concerns of people and culture will be coming to the fore, rather than overly technicist approaches to KM. Our respondents identified with such issues, claiming, for instance, that KM needed to 'legitimate the subject in the eyes of the institutional/professional bodies, and emerging critical managerialist approaches'. This raises the

'**Developments in strategic management over the last
20 years have resulted in a significant challenge to the
orthodox approach to strategy.**'

issue of whether KM will emerge as a distinct academic subject, in the way, for instance, that marketing or human resource management has. Swan (1999) has suggested that while the term KM may well disappear or be replaced by another name, such as organisational knowledge, both the analytical and practical concerns of KM are likely to be an enduring feature of the professional/academic/business environment.

Professor Peter Clark, of the University of Birmingham, has written extensively on the subject of knowledge and organisations. In terms of the emerging KM field, he argues that:

there are too many prescriptive accounts with too little systematic evaluation of concepts against empirical evidence. Sometimes the claims for tacit knowledge represent heroic assumptions … Organisational knowledge as a domain is casually defined and its relationship to knowledge in the wider context is not made clear.

He goes on to point out that KM needs to free itself of the notion that knowledge is an inherently good thing. Rather, he suggests that:

There is considerable anecdotal evidence that suggests existing knowledge, tacit and explicit, can undermine future performance … for instance, Rover possessed extensive tacit knowledge in its occupational communities based in the local district … However, Rover needed to exnovate – to remove – these communities of practice in order to survive. Rover needed to acquire new areas of knowledge. Sadly, the pace of exnovation and innovation in knowledge was too slow.

Strategic management

Developments in strategic management over the last 20 years have resulted in a significant challenge to the orthodox approach to strategy. This is well documented by Whittington (1993). The strategy field, according to Barry and Elmes (1997, p429), is now 'a highly contested and questioned site'. Quinn (1980) began that challenge by questioning the orthodox and somewhat mechanistic approach to planning and implementation. He argued instead for an incremental approach to strategy formulation:

The most effective strategies of major enterprises tend to emerge step-by-step from an iterative process in which the organisation probes the futures, experiments, and learns from a series of partial (incremental) commitments …

(Quinn, 1980, p58).

This opening-up of discussion has led to critiques of the Harvard-based 'design school' for being overly rational – ie constructing abstract models that bear little relation to the reality of strategy. A further critique has been in its concentration on market analysis. The resource-based view (RBV) in strategic management has posed an effective challenge to such thinking, casting aside the preoccupations with market position, segmentation, acquisition and diversification. RB theory has displaced such concerns with a concentration instead on issues such as path dependency, the role of (organisational) history, firm-specific resources, appropriability and politics (Barney, 1991; Collis, 1991; Hall, 1992; Amit and Shoemaker, 1993; Kamoche, 1996; Lado, Boyd and Wright, 1992; Mueller, 1996). The appeal of RBV is that it places emphasis on what the organisation 'can do' as opposed to what Clark (2000, p214) has termed 'the strategic fantasies of formal, written mission statements'. It is this emphasis on what the organisation can do – firm-specific resources – that has led to the interest in understanding how capabilities are produced and maintained. Such concerns have led KM to be placed at the heart of resource-based views of the firm.

Survey findings

- 67% of strategy respondents reported that their institution possessed a KM research centre, one of the centres being a private sector strategy research department.

- Implications for HRM policy and practice:

  - 100% of the sample that were actively researching claimed that their research had implications for recruitment and selection policy and practice.

  - 100% of the sample claimed that their research had implications for training and development in the workplace.

  - 0% of the sample claimed that their KM research had implications for reward and appraisal systems.

  - 50% of the sample claimed that their KM research had implications for organisational and cultural change policy and practice.

  - 50% of the sample claimed that their KM research had implications for organisational design.

- 67% of the sample possessed research funds to investigate KM. Funding sources included

internal university funds and corporate departmental funds.

- 67% of the sample had published articles/book chapters in the field of KM.

Major concerns facing the emerging subject area

Comments here were very mixed, ranging from concerns over academic rigour to the development of the subject base. A sample is provided below:

Bringing rigour into the understanding of the nature of knowledge and knowledge-related processes in organisations, and in its role in organisational performance. Too much emphasis is (currently) on technical/operational aspects.

Developing a distinct identity that takes it beyond organisational learning, managerial and organisational cognition, but which at the same time doesn't become a catch-all area. The field needs a solid academic base, grounded in the base disciplines of the social sciences. To me it is both too broad yet underdeveloped at the same time, spanning cognition, learning knowledge flows, etc. and drawing on not only the mainstream social sciences but also law and the physical, especially engineering, sciences.

We need a clear definition of scope and purpose. A framework for development of the subject – Intellectual Capital Evaluation – let's get it organised and stop it being a red herring. A clear distinction between and juxtaposition of the individual versus organisational knowledge, perhaps, will help progress on Tacit/Explicit interchange too … An ethical framework and justification for the practice of KM in the context of employers and other stakeholders.

In terms of key researchers being identified by scholars in the strategy area, Robert Grant and J.-C. Spender were most frequently mentioned. Anne Huff and Tom Davenport were also cited as being important contributors to the field.

Professor Charles Baden-Fuller, of City University, reflecting on KM from a strategy perspective, commented:

We have a plethora of concepts that suffer from a couple of problems: (first) the definitions are not fixed, and the second difficulty is that they are heuristic, a way of looking at the world, and not models, cause and effect or whatever. There is also a dearth of good empirical work.

In terms of strategic approaches to KM, Baden-Fuller argued that there was a split between essentially static accounts and more dynamic alternatives.

Professor Robert Grant, of Georgetown and City Universities, commented that as a body of thought the development of KM had been illuminating. This was in the sense that it helped differentiate between different types of knowledge rather than just treating knowledge as a 'blanket' term. What it had to offer was that it made explicit many things that were taken for granted. In terms of taking KM further, Grant's view was that there is the possibility of the nascent discipline 'disaggregating' back into the disciplines of IS, HRM, strategy and OS. That said, in his view, an agenda for KM should be attempting to 'look at the implications for developing the principles of organisational design with there being some interesting insights for modularity and the design of teams'. Grant also felt there was an exciting opportunity to look once again at resource-based

theory from a standpoint of combining strategic, HRM and OS perspectives. In substantive terms this was through asking questions such as: 'given resources are turned into capabilities, in part through the use of an organisation's tacit knowledge, how do new firms go about developing such knowledge?' This problem and the role of managerial/HRM action relating to it – ie in developing the requisite resources – are important challenges for KM. Grant framed this interest in empirical terms by posing the question of how Internet start-up companies develop the requisite tacit knowledge to create resources.

Human resource management

The field of human resource management has developed considerably over the last decade, from its incorporation into business schools. Notwithstanding the difficulties experienced by HRM professionals in terms of gaining greater acceptance or increased access to the 'decision space' (cf Whipp and Clark, 1986) within organisations, there has been a profusion of thinking about strategic HRM, which seeks to integrate the operational concerns of HRM – training, recruitment and selection, etc. – into a more strategic perspective (cf Mueller, 1996). The progressive agenda of HRM was problematised in the mid-1990s in the wake of business process re-engineering (BPR), an initiative that was to remove layers of management from organisations (Scarbrough and Burrell, 1996). For HRM, there are lessons to be learned from BPR's neglect of behavioural factors. Although KM arguably represents an attempt to deal with BPR's erosion of the organisational knowledge base, the emphasis on IT in much of the existing literature shows worrying parallels with the BPR experience.

Survey findings

◘ 67% of HRM respondents reported that their institution possessed a KM research centre

◘ Implications for HRM policy and practice:

– 67% of the sample claimed that their research had implications for recruitment and selection policy and practice.

– 100% of the sample claimed that their research had implications for training and development in the workplace.

– 67% of the sample claimed that their KM research had implications for reward and appraisal systems.

– 100% of the sample claimed that their KM research had implications for organisational and cultural change policy and practice.

◘ 100% of the sample possessed research funds to investigate KM. Funding sources included the British ESRC and EPSRC and the Academy of Finland.

◘ 100% of the sample had published articles/ book chapters in the field of KM.

Respondents were reluctant to identify leading centres. Of those that did (33 per cent) in fact reply, Manchester, Warwick, Lancaster and the Open University were mentioned. There was also reticence in naming leading authors. Those who were mentioned were Robert Grant, Ikujiro Nonaka and Hari Tsoukas.

Major concerns facing the emerging subject area

A number of respondents were concerned to delimit the practical scope of KM, for example:

Translating the KM perspective into practice.

Getting beyond the rhetoric to an approach of the practicalities of the issues currently falling under the KM banner, through rigorous empirical work, with an awareness of the relevant psychological as well as strategic issues … A recognition that KM is fundamentally limited in its scope for the analysis of strategic and business issues.

To develop a less individualistic conception of knowledge and knowledge creation – understanding expansive, collective learning and transformation of activities – and to integrate insights from IS, Strategy and HRM for the study of innovation and creation.

Commenting on the reception of KM into HRM debates, Professor Frank Mueller argued that there was a need to make problematic some of the more Utopian assumptions about the sharing of knowledge:

There is always a potentiality of a tension between organisational rationality and individual interests. This is reflected in all areas of HRM activity, such as initial instruction, further development activities, teamworking, quality circles and so on …

In his view, HRM could contribute to the current discourse of KM by highlighting the tensions and trade-offs that exist for organisations. An ambitious programme, Mueller argued, would be to engage with issues surrounding the 'appropriation problem' – ie the problem of capturing the learning of groups and individuals for the benefit of the organisation. In addition, an agenda for KM/HRM would be a better understanding of the knowledge base of an organisation and how the tacit skills or competencies of an employee are in fact activated by the organisation:

The challenge for strategic HRM would be to utilise the localised problem-solving that is going on in specialised teams for the broader vision of the organisation.

Interdisciplinary approaches to KM

The interdisciplinary approach to KM came partly as a result of researchers defining themselves as belonging to, or at least taking concepts from, more than one discipline. In addition, it also referred to researchers who identified themselves as being part of an interdisciplinary research programme. Finally, this group consisted of a few responses from people who belonged to neither of the four disciplines above. Multidisciplinary orientations accounted for around 27 per cent of the total, perhaps a reflection of the growing recognition of the overlaps across different disciplinary boundaries. Within this group some 60 per cent of the respondents were involved in private sector KM research, which was perhaps a reflection that current problems require insights from more than one discipline.

Survey findings

- 60% of respondents reported that their institution possessed a KM research centre.

- Implications for HRM policy and practice:

  - 0% of the sample claimed that their research had implications for recruitment and selection policy and practice.

  - 60% of the sample claimed that their research had implications for training and development in the workplace.

  - 60% of the sample claimed that their KM research had implications for reward and appraisal systems.

  - 80% of the sample claimed that their KM research had implications for organisational and cultural change policy and practice.

- 20% of the sample possessed research funds to investigate KM. Funding sources included the British EPSRC and Department of Trade and Industry.

- 60% of the sample had published articles/book chapters in the field of KM.

Academic centres considered to be at the forefront of research into KM included Harvard, Wharton, Berkeley, Warwick and Cranfield. Leading authors on KM included Robert Grant, Nonaka, Dorothy Leonard, David Snowden, Tom Davenport and Jay Liebowitz.

Major concerns facing the emerging subject area

There was a general impetus here towards a more sophisticated analysis and application of KM, both at individual and organisational level. For example:

We need an efficient method for understanding the detailed human factors behind each type of knowledge exchange a person in a role needs to undertake. This is particularly important in creative or problem-solving tasks such as design.

Understanding and communicating what knowledge should be captured before sharing and what knowledge should remain tacit for sharing. What are the criteria that enable us to identify which approach is appropriate?

Defining a useful intervention to improve knowledge capture, sharing and reuse; and then monitoring its effectiveness.

There is a danger that KM might become too simplistic (ie driven solely by technology) or too esoteric or philosophical (with little perceived benefit to practising managers).

Establishing the clarity and the boundary of the field.

The discipline is full of companies wishing to sell consulting services or IT services and missing the key issue of cultural change.

Professor Paul Quintas, of the Open University Business School, summarised the challenges for the future of KM:

Sustaining credibility for the subject in the face of commercial and technology hype; sustaining interest from practitioners and policy makers who require quick fixes; the development of sufficiently rich interdisciplinary conceptual frameworks; the development of theory; the difficulty of developing research methods that can address complex issues such as tacit knowledge.

Summary findings

In the sections above, the concerns of particular disciplinary groupings have been presented. This section aggregates the survey in order to present some overall findings.

◻ 59% of respondents reported that their institution possessed a KM research centre.

◻ 41% of the sample possessed research funds to investigate KM. Funding sources included the British ESRC and EPSRC, the DTI, the Academy of Finland, the Swedish Government, the European Union, university sponsorship and corporate sponsorship.

◻ Implications for HRM policy and practice:

   – 27% of the sample claimed that their research had implications for recruitment and selection policy and practice.

   – 63% of the sample claimed that their research had implications for training and development in the workplace.

   – 27% of the sample claimed that their KM research had implications for reward and appraisal systems.

   – 77% of the sample claimed that their KM research had implications for organisational and cultural change policy and practice.

◻ 72% of the sample had published articles/book chapters in the field of KM.

> '**The most immediate conclusion to be drawn from this questionnaire is that KM has burgeoned as an area of academic enquiry.**'

Academic centres considered to be at the forefront of research into KM included: UMIST, Warwick, Lancaster, the Open University, Cranfield, Sheffield, Harvard, Wharton, California San Diego and California Berkeley. In terms of the most important authors contributing to KM, 37 per cent of the sample declined to answer, whether considering the field too disparate or not being willing to be drawn on the issue. Of the 63 per cent who did name authors, these consisted of, in no particular order: Van Krogh, Nonaka, Davenport, Blackler, Hamel, Barton, Spender, Snowden, Seely-Brown, Skyrme, Tsoukas, Wenger, Huff, Eden, Grant, Liebowitz and Shadbolt.

Discussion of the questionnaire findings

The most immediate conclusion to be drawn from this questionnaire is that KM has burgeoned as an area of academic enquiry. The questionnaire, while limited in its scope, has important implications for KM and HRM. It seems to send a mixed message about the current focus of research in the KM field. On the one hand, as our findings show, the HRM concerns of organisational culture and change, and training and development are held to be of particular importance to the KM debate. Yet, on the other hand, despite the widespread acknowledgement of the importance of HRM, it remains unclear how far HRM issues are actually a central element of much of the existing research. In many instances, our survey responses suggest that HRM factors are viewed as important contextual variables, but secondary factors in the research design. Also, a smaller percentage of researchers identified themselves as working within the HRM discipline, and none of the 'leading scholars' listed in the study could be readily described as being HRM academics. Given the ready evidence of the emergence of KM as an academic research area, supported by research

grants and sustained within specialist research centres engaged in the production of academic articles and books, this suggests some risk that HRM may be marginalised in research on KM.

These comments should not be read as a sweeping generalisation or as criticism of extant work on KM. Rather, mindful of the potential significance of HRM, as identified by researchers themselves, it can be regarded as defining a window of opportunity that requires a response from advocates of HRM. The 'HRM gap' in current research underlines the importance of developing a meaningful dialogue between HRM thinkers and other disciplinary groups if the field is to move towards a research agenda that properly addresses the implications for HRM.

Moving away from the specific concerns of HRM, the research findings clearly highlight a number of challenges. Most fundamental is the question of whether the current enthusiasm for KM will be sustained, and whether this will result in the long-term development of a KM discipline. The latter seems to depend, from our survey responses, on the emergence of a greater degree of consensus over theory, in combination with the development of research methodologies to investigate many of the problematic intangibles of knowledge.

Knowledge management research centres

This section will present an overview of existing research activities broken down by centre, themes and disciplinary context (eg strategy or organisational behaviour, academic or practitioner-oriented). It will be hyperlinked to researchers' accounts of their work on institutional websites. The primary focus will be work in the UK, but we shall also address major research groupings in the

USA and Europe. We begin by highlighting the major research programmes currently being conducted into KM, and follow this by an overview of different KM research institutions.

Major research programmes in knowledge management

UK ESRC's (Economic and Social Research Council) Innovation Programme

One important set of research studies that has important KM implications is the major programme of research on innovation funded by the UK's ESRC. This programme, which has recently ended, involved the funding of a large number of research studies in UK universities concerned with the management of innovation. A number of these studies incorporated elements of KM in their brief, as outlined below.

Knowledge Management Practices: Rod Coombs and Richard Hull, UMIST

This study focused on the management of Research and Development (R&D) staff through case study research in five different UK R&D organisations. The study identified over 80 KM practices (KMPs) under five major headings:

1   KMPs in the formal management process – including the documentation and reporting of projects, etc.

2   Mapping knowledge relationships – eg gathering information on the strategic R&D alliances of competitors.

3   Managing intellectual property – practices for exploiting patents, etc.

4   HRM for R&D employees – eg KM objectives being reflected in reward and appraisal systems such as PRP.

5   KMPs and IT – the use of IT systems to communicate knowledge.

Key findings: While R&D organisations have always conducted some form of KM, this has traditionally focused on the storage, documentation and transmission of knowledge within a particular innovation project. There has been little attempt to share knowledge across projects. This is important, however, as the accretion of knowledge from projects determines the cumulative development of a firm's innovation capability.

The study also produced an 'audit tool' for evaluating KM practices in R&D. This is available from the research centre's website at: http://nt2.ec.man.ac.uk/usercgi/cric/cricpaperdl.asp

Management of Intellectual Capital for Innovation: Paul Quintas et al, MKIRU, Open University Business School

The main aim of this study was to determine whether the looser employment relationships required by flexibility strategies would undermine or stimulate an organisation's innovative capability. It involved a survey of 2700 firms and eight case studies.

Key findings: The study found that in the sample firms innovation was not a systemic or an organisation-wide activity. It was seen as involving only a specific section of the workforce. Despite this, there was some evidence that a high-commitment employment strategy was linked to innovation. The spread of flexible employment

> 'The most valuable rewards to motivate employee
> innovation are accelerated promotion, flexible working,
> a dual career track and one-off bonuses to individuals.'

practices, however, applied mainly to employees not regarded as key to the innovation process.

The study identified three types of link between employment flexibility and innovation:

- Decoupled – casualised employment of some workers has no impact on innovation.

- Semi-coupled – new flexibly employed staff liberate existing staff to become more involved in innovation.

- Close coupling – new flexible employees engender novel approaches or reduce the cost of access to specialist expertise.

The study confirmed previous work that suggested that customers are important sources of innovation. However, the development of tighter business network relationships was leading to the short-circuiting of supply chains – middlemen were being cut out.

The study concluded that UK firms underutilise their intellectual capital. They could do more to involve the expertise of all employees in innovation projects. Also, they could learn more from the consultants and temporary staff they employ.

E-mail: p.quintas@open.ac.uk

Innovation and Reward: Marc Thompson, Ian Kessler and Paul Heron, Templeton College, Oxford University

This study examined the role of reward strategies in encouraging employees to be innovative. The study focused on R&D employees in the high-tech sector. Reward was defined broadly to include pay and benefits, intrinsic job satisfaction and occupational status. Two different types of reward strategy were examined:

1 Transactional strategies: centred on the use of incentives, such as individual performance pay and greater risk-sharing and a flexible pay structure, which emphasise short-term, monetary exchanges, with strong explicit linkages between outputs and rewards.

2 Relational strategies: emphasise long-term time horizons, stress the importance of employee involvement in the process of strategy development and provide an organisational context in which this can happen – the pay system design is decentralised to operating units ensuring fit.

Key findings: Firms with relational reward strategies had higher levels of innovative performance. These firms were also more likely to invest in job design. It could be argued that higher levels of innovative performance (measured by managerial judgement of comparative performance on several innovation dimensions) is a proxy measure of knowledge utilisation.

The most valuable rewards to motivate employee innovation are accelerated promotion, flexible working, a dual career track and one-off bonuses to individuals. Less highly rated are profit-sharing incentives, such as employee share ownership schemes. Least highly rated are financial rewards for published papers and sabbaticals.

E-mail: marc.thompson@templeton.oxford.ac.uk

Knowledge management institutions

United Kingdom

In this section we present a summary of major centres for the study of knowledge management in British academia. As far as possible this listing uses the self-descriptions of specific institutions in terms of their relationship to KM.

The explosion of interest in KM has been mirrored by its rise within UK business schools. KM is currently being researched by academics from a diverse range of disciplines, with organisation studies, strategy and information systems being the most prevalent. This section seeks to highlight the key areas of research activity in the UK. Every attempt has been made to ensure that this is a robust if not forensic account. This has entailed an analysis of journal articles, conference proceedings and details of ongoing research programmes.

Aston University

The KM research group at Aston Business School comprises the members from the former information systems group. It is part of the larger operations and information management group. This is reflected in its research interests. It has recently organised a major conference on KM. Key members of the KM group are John Kidd and John Edwards.

Key publications: van der Spek R., Edwards J. S., Mallis R., van der Meij B. F. and Taylor R. M. (1999). 'Investigating a theoretical framework for Knowledge Management: a gaming approach', in Liebowitz J (ed.), *The Knowledge Management Handbook* (pp10–1 to 10–18). Boca Raton, FL, CRC Press.

Birmingham University

Knowledge and innovation is researched in the Department of Commerce by Professors Peter Clark and Jennifer Tann. The management of knowledge was a central theme of Professor Clark's latest book. Professor John Child, formerly of the Judge Institute at Cambridge, is currently working on a book with Nonaka.

Key publications: Clark P. (2000) *Organisations in Action*. London, Routledge.

Brighton University

The CENTRIM group at Brighton University is involved in collaborative work on KM with SPRU of Sussex University. Their current EPSRC project is investigating 'Improving performance in complex product systems production via inter-project knowledge capture and transfer'. The aim of this research is to improve the performance of organisations involved in the development and production of complex product systems and to contribute to the theoretical understanding of knowledge management practices in project-based organisations.

Cambridge University, Judge Institute of Management Studies

Research into KM is currently conducted by Chong Ju Choi and Professor Geoff Walsham. In broad terms, they take an IS approach to KM but also examine the implications of communities of practice. Within the organisation studies group Chris Grey has conducted a number of studies into the ambiguities and complexities of knowledge work, especially in relation to the socialisation of chartered accountants.

Key publications: Hayes, N and Walsham G. (2000) 'Safe enclaves, political enclaves and knowledge working', pp69–87, in Prichard C., Hull R., Chumer H. and Willmott H. (eds), *Managing Knowledge: Critical investigations of work and learning*. London, Macmillan.

City University

City has acted as a forum for the development of theories such as the 'knowledge-based theory of the firm' and 'knowledge-based competition' that seek to help understand what they describe as models of 'disproportionate competition and knowledge management'. In particular, City has strengths in the strategic management approach to KM. City itself identifies four members of faculty possessing expertise in KM: Professor Keith Bradley concentrates on the application of KM and intellectual capital; Professor Rob Grant has written some of the seminal work on KM and strategy; Professor Charles Baden-Fuller is currently working on 'knowledge management in newly emerging markets (bio-technology)'; Professor Clive Holtham is actively involved in the Financial Services Knowledge Laboratory.

A recent study included a commission by the Design Council into knowledge and organisations. While there was no evidence of research funding, it was clear that KM researchers had extensive contact with organisations through their consulting activities. Professor Charles Baden-Fuller is chief editor of *Long Range Planning* journal, which recently ran a special issue on KM.

Key publications: Grant R. and Baden-Fuller C. (1999) 'Firms, markets and alliances and the efficiency of knowledge application', in Von Krogh G. and Nonaka I. (eds), *Knowledge Management*. London, Macmillan.

Grant R.M. and Spender J.C. (1996) 'Knowledge and the firm: overview'. *Strategic Management Journal*, Vol. 17, Winter Special Issue, pp5–10.

Grant R.M. (1996) 'Towards a knowledge-based theory of the firm'. *Strategy Management Journal*, Vol. 17, Winter Special Issue, pp109–122.

Cranfield University

The information systems group at Cranfield University has recently published the widely promoted 'European Knowledge Management Survey'. This survey attempts to identify 'Europe's State of the Art in Knowledge Management'. The survey was conducted in collaboration with Xerox and Information Strategy. It argues that European organisations, in order to fully exploit their knowledge, need both a change in culture and different tools. In addition, Cranfield have also recently published the Microsoft survey of UK Knowledge Management. The key finding of this report was to highlight that while the benefits of KM are recognised at an abstract level, they are not feeding into effective implementation in the workplace. Ashley Braganza and Rob Lambert, of Cranfield School of Management, are currently preparing a special issue of the *Journal of Knowledge and Process Management* that is building on their current work.

Durham University

Research into KM at Durham Business School is being conducted by Pierpaolo Andriani and Professor Richard Hall. The former is investigating the existence of knowledge in industrial clusters, while the latter has published important work on valuing intangible assets in organisations and is currently carrying out research into KM and supply chain management.

Key publications: Hall R. (1992) 'The strategic analysis of intangible resources'. *Strategic Management Journal*, Vol. 13, pp135–144.

Kent University

Dr Alice Lam, Reader at the Management Centre at the University of Kent, is primarily concerned with investigating societal differences in relation to the management of knowledge in different nations. She has studied the constellation of relationships between national culture, the dominant form of knowledge in an organisation and organisational design.

Key publications: Lam A. (1997) 'Embedded firms, embedded knowledge: problems of collaboration and knowledge transfer in global cooperative ventures'. *Organisation Studies*, Vol. 8, No. 6, pp973–996.

Kings College, London

The recent appointment of David Guest brings to Kings College a research programme investigating issues concerning the psychological contract in the workplace and the questions this raises for KM. His findings highlight the need for an organisation to gain the trust of employees if KM initiatives are to enjoy the support of the workforce. David Guest has research grants from the ESRC Innovation Programme and from the Chartered Institute of Personnel and Development.

Key publications: Guest D. (1998) 'Beyond HRM: commitment and the contract culture', in Sparrow P. and Marchington M. (eds), *Human Resource Management: The new agenda*. London, Financial Times Management.

Lancaster University, Management School

The University of Lancaster has long-standing strengths in management learning. A number of this cohort have made important contributions to the KM debate. For instance, Professor Frank Blackler has fruitfully applied activity-based theory to routines of knowledge in the workplace (see below). Professors Easterby-Smith and Burgoyne are influential commentators on management and organisational learning.

Key publications: Blackler F. (1995) 'Knowledge, knowledge work and organisations: an overview and interpretation'. *Organisation Studies* . Vol. 16, No. 6, pp1021–1046.

Leicester University

The University of Leicester's Management Centre is the host for a major academic and practitioner conference: 'Managing Knowledge: Conversations and Critiques', to be held on 10–11 April 2001.

Website: http://www.le.ac.uk/lumc/ kmconf2000.html

London School of Economics

KM is firmly rooted within the information systems division at the LSE, a division that places great emphasis on the social features of technology. In terms of individual contribution, the recently assembled group has made a distinctive contribution to understanding the role of technology and IS in KM. Key contributors to the group include Professor Claudio Ciborra, Edgar Whitley, Carsten Sorensen and Professor Bob Galliers.

Key publications: Ciborra C. and Patriotta G. (1996) 'Groupware and teamwork in new product development: The case of a consumer goods multinational', in Ciborra C. (ed.), *Groupware and Teamwork*. New York, Wiley.

Nottingham Trent University

Professor Sue Newell has produced work questioning the role of information systems in KM. In addition to this, Professor Newell is currently working on the implications of KM for HRM with particular reference to selection and assessment.

Key publications: Newell S. (1995) *The Healthy Organisation*. London, Routledge.

Open University

Since 1996, the Managing Knowledge and Innovation Research Unit (MKIRU) has been investigating issues around knowledge management. The Open University has in the last 18 months made a number of KM appointments. The core team is Paul Quintas, formerly of SPRU and the UK's first Professor of Knowledge Management, John Storey, Steve Little and Tim Ray (who worked with Nonaka in Japan). They are currently compiling a book of readings on KM to be published by Sage. The Open University Business School has also developed a major KM module in its MBA programme.

Key publications: Quintas P., Lefrere P. and Jones G. (1997) 'Knowledge management: a strategic agenda'. *Long Range Planning*. Vol. 30, No. 3, pp385–391.

Strathclyde University

Professor Paul Thompson and Chris Warhurst are conducting empirical research into knowledge

work and service work, developing a critical perspective on the competencies involved in such settings. Professor Hari Tsoukas has recently taken up a visiting appointment at the university.

Key publications: Thompson P., Warhurst C. and Callaghan G. (2000) 'Human capital or capitalising on humanity?' pp122–140 in Prichard C., Hull R., Chumer H. and Willmott H. (eds), *Managing Knowledge: Critical investigations of work and learning*. London, Macmillan.

Tsoukas H. (1996) 'The firm as a distributed knowledge system: a constructionist approach'. *Strategic Management Journal*. Vol. 17, Special Issue, pp11–25.

St Andrews University

Alan McKinlay has developed a perspective on KM which highlights the role of power, surveillance and reflexivity.

Key publications: McKinlay A. (2000) 'The bearable lightness of control: organisational reflexivity and the politics of knowledge management', pp107–121 in Prichard C., Hull R., Chumer H. and Willmott H. (eds), *Managing Knowledge: Critical investigations of work and learning*. London, Macmillan.

Sussex University

The Science Policy Research Unit (SPRU) is world famous for its contributions to technology debates. Mike Gibbons, lead author of the seminal 'New Production of Knowledge' was at SPRU while he conducted the studies. Key figures at SPRU include Keith Pavitt. The unit's current research into KM is in conjunction with the University of Brighton.

Key publications: Pavitt K. (1998) 'Technologies, products and organisation in the innovating firm: what Adam Smith tells us and Joseph Schumpeter doesn't'. *Industrial and Corporate Change*. Vol. 7, pp433–452.

UMIST

Research into KM at UMIST has been conducted by Professor Rod Coombs, who, as described above, has been involved in developing a KM audit tool. Professor Hugh Willmott is also involved in KM research in terms of investigating knowledge work, especially in terms of its inextricable links with issues of power. Professor Willmott is also currently researching into the 'Millennium Bug' as an example of the social construction of knowledge, performance measures and emergent outcomes.

Key publications: Coombs R. and Hull R. (1998) 'Knowledge management practices and path dependency'. *Research Policy*. Vol. 27, pp237–253.

Prichard C., Hull R., Chumer H. and Willmott H. (1998) (eds), *Managing Knowledge: Critical investigations of work and learning*. London, Macmillan.

Warwick University

Warwick Business School provides a base for IKON, the inter-university research unit for Innovation, Knowledge and Organisational Networks. At present, IKON is conducting research into cross-sectoral knowledge capture, funded by the EPSRC. Key members of IKON are Jacky Swan, Sue Newell and Maxine Robertson. Under the auspices of the Business Process Resource Centre, Warwick was host to this year's inaugural Knowledge Management: Concepts and Controversies conference.

Website: http://users.wbs.warwick.ac.uk/ikon/

Key publications: Swan J., Newell S., Scarbrough H. and Hislop D. (1999) 'Knowledge management and innovation; networks and networking'. *Journal of Knowledge Management*. Vol. 3, No. 4, pp262–275.

North America

Shifting our attention towards North America, it is important to reiterate that the time of the year when this study was conducted, combined with the timescale, makes this account somewhat more concise than the above on the UK. The objectives in this section are somewhat less ambitious. The aim is to provide a brief account of significant centres for the study of KM in the USA.

University of California, Berkeley

Professor David Teece, at the Haas School of Business at the University of California, has made a substantial contribution to understandings of intangible assets and markets for know-how.

Harvard Business School

Research at Harvard Business School into KM has taken place primarily through the work of Professor Dorothy Leonard. She has published extensively on the subject of KM. In particular, she has worked on issues surrounding the development and exploitation of knowledge assets. A second area of interest is investigation into the role that the sharing of tacit knowledge plays in new product development. Third, Professor Leonard has investigated the process of creativity in the innovation process.

Key publications: Leonard D. and Swap W. (1999) *When Sparks Fly: Igniting creativity in groups*. Cambridge, MA, Harvard Business School Press.

Leonard-Barton D. (1998) *Wellsprings of Knowledge: Building and sustaining the sources of innovation*. Boston, Harvard Business School Press (first published 1995, reissued in paperback 1998).

North Eastern University

Michael Zack, of North Eastern, has published widely on the subject of KM.

Key publication: Zack M. 'Developing a knowledge strategy'. *California Management Review*. Vol. 41, No. 3, Spring 1999, pp125–145

Stanford University School of Business

Academic work into KM is currently being conducted by Professor Jeffrey Pfeffer, who is perhaps more famous for his work on power and politics in organisations.

Key publications: Pfeffer J. and Sutton R.J. (2000) *The Knowing-Doing Gap: How smart companies turn knowledge into action*. Cambridge, MA, Harvard Business School Press.

Stern School of Business, New York University

Raghu Garud and Professor Bill Starbuck are both working in the KM area.

Wharton School of Business, University of Pennsylvania

Wharton School's contribution to KM has been predominantly through its department of management, which includes Professor Bruce Kogut (whose website is http://www.wharton.upenn.edu/faculty/kogut.html), who has made a significant contribution to the KM debate. Active researchers include Anne Marie

Knott, who is working on the development of an 'interactive agent model of knowledge creation and diffusion as means to reconcile competing perspectives of sociology and economics on knowledge flow' (http://www.wharton.upenn.edu/faculty/knott.html); Gabriel Szulanski, who is examining economic rent appropriation through knowledge utilisation; and Mark J. Zbaracki, who is examining applications of business knowledge.

Europe

ESADE, Barcelona

Professor Max Boisot of ESADE has published extensively on the subject of knowledge. He has made theoretical contributions as well as detailed empirical studies of the Chinese business system.

Key publications: Boisot M. (1995) *Information Space*. London, Routledge. Boisot M. (1998) *Knowledge Assets: Securing competitive advantage in the information economy*. Oxford, Oxford University Press.

Aix-en-Provence, France

Phillippe Baumard at Aix-en-Provence has made a significant contribution to the study of tacit knowledge. He has undertaken a number of rich empirical case studies that have sought to develop a more nuanced account of tacit knowledge.

Key publications: Baumard P. (1998) *Tacit Knowledge*. London, Sage.

University of Lund, Sweden

Work into KM is being conducted at the University of Lund by Professor Mats Alvesson and Dan Karreman. At an abstract level, their work has sought to deconstruct and problematise some of the assumptions that are taken as axiomatic in KM. Professor Alvesson has also made a significant contribution to understandings of knowledge work, through drawing attention to issues of image and rhetoric intensity and their importance in situations of inherent ambiguity.

Key publications: Alvesson M. (1995) *Management of Knowledge-Intensive Companies*. Berlin/New York, Walter De Gruyter.

Australia

University of Technology, Sydney

Thomas Clarke, of UTS, is presently engaged in research into KM. More generally, the organisation studies group at UTS has made a distinctive contribution to understandings of the production and diffusion of managerial initiatives.

New Zealand

Massey University

Craig Prichard, of Massey University, researches into knowledge and knowledge work.

Key publications: Prichard C., Hull R., Chumer H. and Willmott H. (1998) (eds), *Managing Knowledge: Critical investigations of work and learning*. London, Macmillan.

Writers on knowledge management

In the findings presented above, a number of writers were cited as having made an 'important' contribution to the KM discussion. In the section below we attempt to capture concisely the central features of each author's work. An attempt will

then be made to consider, where applicable, the potential implications of their position for HRM theory and practice.

Professor Robert Grant

Professor Robert Grant, of City University, London and Georgetown, Washington DC, has been one of the pioneers of the resource-based (RB) approach to strategy. RB theory in essence marked a break with previous market-based approaches to strategy. It has been termed the 'inside-out' view of strategy, as opposed to the outside-in view. In the last decade it has become a highly influential approach to the analysis of strategy. The suggestion is that rather than deploying elaborate tools that seek to evaluate the market position, plan a segmentation strategy, or take decisions to acquire or diversify, strategists should rather look internally to the organisation and ask the question 'what is it that the organisation can actually do?' Part of the rationale for this RB approach is that in turbulent and fast-moving market conditions it makes little sense to orient the whole strategy of an organisation towards a fixed view of a market, which by its very nature is likely to change. The RB approach suggests that examining the capabilities of a firm offers a better starting point for the development of a strategy. The crux of this approach is that if firms can mobilise their resources, they can create firm-specific capabilities that are a potential source of competitive advantage.

Mobilising resources into capabilities is seen as a critical role for management. Central to such an analysis is the possibility that the executives in an organisation may not actually be aware of where the organisational capabilities lie. Grant's analysis is an attempt to engage with the 'how' of the translation of resources into capabilities. He draws from Edith Penrose's seminal early work on tacit knowledge, in terms of trying to make sense of the complex interaction between tacit and explicit knowledge. Penrose's model of learning emphasises the role of the knowledge of experience; something that is in contrast to notions of objective, explicit knowledge. Grant is interested in the role of experiential learning, viewing it as tacit expertise that is physically embodied in employees.

The implications of Grant's position for HRM are twofold. In the first place, he emphasises the ways HRM can assist in sustaining capabilities: through operational policies, such as retaining and developing staff, but also through the more strategic identification of the actual capabilities, and how they might be charted. A more fundamental challenge for HRM is developing organisational capabilities from resources. This is clearly not an easy question. Professor Grant's current work into dot.com start-ups is an attempt to explore the mechanisms through which tacit knowledge is created.

Janine Nahapiet

Janine Nahapiet, a Fellow at Templeton College, University of Oxford, has collaborated with Professor Ghoshal of London Business School in highlighting the relationships between social and intellectual capital. Their argument contends that organisations are 'conducive to the creation of new intellectual capital' (1998, p242), and that this can in part be achieved through the use of social capital. Social capital is said to be greater within organisations than markets because of the denseness and repeated exchanges that are a commonplace part of organisational life.

The application of social capital to KM mirrors a broader view that has seen social capital being increasingly used as an explanatory concept to explain issues as diverse as economic performance at the level of the firm, the region and the nation. Nahapiet and Ghoshal's argument is that social capital 'constitutes a valuable resource for the conduct of social affairs' (p243).

Nahapiet's view is that social capital when combined and exchanged with intellectual capital leads to the creation of fresh intellectual capital that may result in a competitive advantage for an organisation. She argues that 'it is the coevolution of social and intellectual capital that is of particular significance in explaining the source of organisational advantage'. This faith in social capital has led to the construction of a finely grained operationalisation of the concept in order to understand it in greater detail. In many respects this is a synthesis of many disparate writings on social networks.

The implications for HRM of Nahapiet's work are both challenging and potentially wide ranging. To accept her thesis is to elevate social capital as pivotal to the creation of intellectual capital. The analytical problem for HRM becomes, therefore, how should the creation and maintenance of social capital be managed? Moreover, how would this be managed in such a way as to foster an environment whereby there are opportunities for the combination and exchange of intellectual capital? In such an environment, people expect this will be a useful activity; they will be motivated to engage in such activity, ie in terms of trust; and finally there will be sufficient common understandings to facilitate the sharing of ideas. This is clearly a huge challenge for HRM, one that has profound implications for the role and status of HRM within organisations. And while Nahapiet's work has not directly dealt with such concerns, she has noted the tendency for knowledge-intensive firms:

… to invest heavily in resources, including physical facilities, to encourage the development of strong personal and team relationships, high levels of personal trust, norm-based control, and strong connections across porous boundaries (1998, p260).

By way of a caveat, while Nahapiet has argued powerfully for the importance of social capital, its manageability remains open to question. Rather, it may prove to be a phenomenon that proves to be resolutely part of the 'informal' organisation, resistant to managerial interventions. A further point is that it would be a misrepresentation of Nahapiet to argue that social capital is *per se* a good thing; rather, she notes that it might in some circumstances inhibit the goals of an organisation.

Key publication: Nahapiet J. and Ghoshal S. (1998) 'Social capital, intellectual capital and the organisational advantage'. *Academy of Management Review*. Vol. 23, No. 2, pp242–266.

Jacky Swan

Dr Jacky Swan, of Warwick Business School, Coventry, is one of the founder members of the IKON research group, and is a Reader in Organisation Studies. Dr Swan has made a substantial contribution to the literature on the diffusion of innovation. These interests in the diffusion and then implementation of innovations were broadly theorised through the analytical apparatus of the Decision Episode framework, which has been refined as a result of the findings. The diffusion/implementation work extended to studies of early iterations of knowledge management in a pan-European study. The findings, some of which were published by the CIPD, have significant implications for the theory and practice of KM, for the studies chronicle 'good, mad and bad' implementations. In particular, they chart the implementation of company intranets, which for many organisations are synonymous with KM. Put simply, in some cases the lack of a strategy led to the confusing proliferation of different intranets within organisations. Moreover, in another case an intranet was regarded as a solution to KM without any detailed consideration of the people issues associated with technology. Dr Swan has argued for the need for a contextually based approach to KM that addresses the people issues involved.

Subsequent to the study, Jacky Swan has pursued this interest by investigating the foundations of the theoretical approaches to KM. She has empirically demonstrated the way in which KM as an academic discipline has been dominated by information systems, which, looking as it does through the lens of technology, downplays the importance of people issues. This tendency runs the risk of foreshortening the life of KM, if it is to be limited to the introduction of technological 'solutions' that are not only expensive but also in themselves problematic.

A further research interest pursued by Swan is an investigation of KM as management fashion. In developing her corporate fashion thesis, she demonstrates how there has been an explosion of interest in KM over the last few years. She furthers the argument that this can in part be explained

> 'In terms of the 'priorities for knowledge management', Blackler argues that in emergent and uncertain situations there is a challenge for KM to facilitate development and collaboration.'

through 'mimetic isomorphism', which means the tendency of organisations to copy so-called 'leading' organisations. This raises the question of whether, like the quality and BPR movements, KM will fade from the corporate consciousness. Swan contends that while the term 'knowledge management' may disappear, the concerns of managing knowledge are likely to be an enduring part of the problems faced by organisations in the future.

Professor Frank Blackler

Professor Frank Blackler, of Lancaster University, is well known for his work into learning in organisations. He is currently an important contributor to the debate on KM. Like many of his organisation studies colleagues, he argues that there are fundamental problems with the reification of knowledge (treating it as an object) outside its context of application. For Blackler, it is far more useful to displace 'knowledge' with the notion of 'knowing', ie a concept that captures the sense of activities consisting of objects, people and systems. Activity theory, drawing from the work of the Russian psychologist Vygotsky, seeks to emphasise the relationships between 'knowing, material artefacts and power'. Activity theory highlights the precarious, tentative nature of knowing – as opposed to the certainties of knowledge. Moreover, it attempts to inject a sense of process into understanding what happens in particular organisational situations.

Intrinsic to this perspective is the notion that 'activity systems are historical, multifaceted, collective, multi-voiced and developing … while actions are transient, activities are relatively enduring' (Blackler, 2000, p2). The tentative nature of knowing can, however, be obscured by the apparent immutability of objectified knowledge. It

is Blackler's position that knowledge does not transcend time and space, and that all claims on knowledge are in essence contestable. In terms of the 'priorities for knowledge management', Blackler argues that in emergent and uncertain situations there is a challenge for KM to facilitate development and collaboration.

The implications for HRM of Blackler's work are twofold. First, applying activity theory to an agenda for HRM would be to recognise that dominant representations of KM – those that are silent on the subject of HRM – are contestable and challengeable. Second, in terms of HRM playing a greater role in KM, the challenge would be for HRM to facilitate knowledge-sharing and creation through the development of policies that specifically address activities rather than merely attempting to codify knowledge. In addition to his role as a theorist looking at knowledge, Blackler has also made it clear that KM needs a second generation that marks a substantive shift away from its current concerns.

Professor Ikujiro Nonaka

Professor Ikujiro Nonaka is widely regarded as the doyen of knowledge management. His co-authored book (with Hirotaka Takeuchi), The Knowledge Creating Company is a management best-seller and is arguably the anchor point for KM. Nonaka's major contribution, other than highlighting the importance of knowledge in organisations, was to introduce a framework for the study of knowledge. He argued that knowledge is either tacit or explicit (his epistemological dimension), and is held at the level of either the individual or the collective (his ontological dimension). By opening up these distinctions, Nonaka is able to construct a 2 x 2 matrix, which enables him to locate where knowledge resides, and what characteristics it possesses. From this point, he is able to makes propositions with regard to the translation of one form of knowledge to another. He argues that there are 'four modes of knowledge conversion' (p62): (i) tacit to tacit (Socialisation); (ii) explicit to tacit (Internalisation); (iii) explicit to explicit (Combination); and (iv) what Nonaka and Takeuchi argue is the 'quintessential form of knowledge conversion' when tacit is turned into explicit knowledge (Externalisation).

It is the externalisation of tacit into explicit knowledge that is the very essence of much of what is being attempted in KM programmes. This can be seen through initiatives such as the construction of corporate intranets and the like. Nonaka assumes therefore that knowledge can be transformed from one form, tacit, into another, explicit. According to Nonaka: 'organisational knowledge creation is a continuous and dynamic interaction between tacit and explicit knowledge. This interaction is shaped by shifts between different modes of knowledge conversion' (p70).

For knowledge creation to take place, Nonaka contends that the most effective type of management model can be characterised as 'middle-up-down'. Broadly speaking, this signifies an organisation whereby the chief 'agent of knowledge creation' is the team; the role of top management is to act as a catalyst; and the middle management role is that of team leader. The middle-up-down model facilitates the combination of tacit and explicit knowledge that creates a knowledge spiral. This organisational design operates as a 'hypertext', ie a combination of hierarchy and project teams. Moreover, communication is through conversation and through the deployment of metaphors and analogies. Nonaka conjectures that the advantages

of this form of organisation are in its ability to deal with ambiguity and to create knowledge. Its disadvantage is the work intensity and stress created for employees.

Professor Max Boisot

Professor Max Boisot, of ESADE, Barcelona, has approached knowledge from the perspective of strategic management. He takes as his starting point the notion that the management of knowledge is a fundamental requirement for securing competitive advantage. He has developed a theory of 'Information Space' (I-Space) with which to explore knowledge and organisations. In the development of his I-Space framework Boisot starts from first principles. He suggests that the dimensions of I-Space revolve around the continua of codified-uncodified, abstract-concrete and diffused-undiffused knowledge, that are capable of being integrated into a single three-dimensional framework. Boisot goes on to describe the movement of knowledge within I-Space. This is a process that he terms the 'social-learning cycle', something akin to double loop learning. In essence this is a six-stage process that commences with 'scanning' – identifying threats and opportunities (1998, p59) – and ends with 'impacting' – the 'embedding of abstract knowledge in concrete practices' (1998, p61). According to Boisot, the social learning cycle is a means of representing 'knowledge flows'. His I-Space framework can also be employed to represent knowledge assets – 'assets are stocks rather than flows and we have seen that knowledge assets can be stocked in people's heads, in documents, or in artefacts' (1998, p63). The argument is that an organisation's capability, or in other words its distinctive, firm-specific assets, can be schematically presented in I-Space: 'a firm's distinctive competence could now appear as a unique configuration of knowledge assets embedded in goods, documents, or the minds of agents, located in different regions of the I-Space and organisationally integrated to deliver superior performance' (1998, p255).

Moving from the detail of the I-Space model to a broader contextualisation, in the wake of the information revolution Boisot argues that the objectives of traditional management, which were among other things to reduce uncertainty, 'are no longer the only recipes on offer for the creation of competitive firms' (p265). Instead he outlines the new managerial challenge as being able to create organisations capable of absorbing, as opposed to reducing, uncertainty.

Professor Claudio Ciborra, Professor of Information Systems, London School of Economics

Professor Ciborra is one of the leading European thinkers on information systems and has sought to incorporate management and organisational issues within the discipline (Ciborra, 1993). A particular contribution has been the critique of attempts to apply formal, rational planning methods to the design and use of systems. Ciborra highlights the importance of 'drift' in the use of systems and the role of local initiatives and tactical usage. He argues that 'strategic' uses of IS often emerge from these local experiments and adaptations. These insights have been applied to a number of the tools developed to aid KM, in particular groupware packages such as Lotus Notes. This shows that the final use of these systems depends heavily upon the local context and responses of users and is not readily managed in a top-down way (Ciborra and Patriotta, 1996).

Professor J.-C. Spender, Dean of Business and Technology, State University of New York

Spender has made a number of important contributions to our understanding of knowledge in organisations. These include his seminal work on the strategic 'recipes' that developed within industrial sectors (1989). Latterly, Spender's work has focused on a critique of positivist approaches to organisational knowledge – the notion that knowledge can be viewed unproblematically as an asset. Instead, he has sought to complement the distinction between tacit and explicit knowledge with an understanding of the implications of individual and collective forms of knowledge (Spender, 1996).
Website: http://www.fitnyc.suny.edu/

Professor Haridimos Tsoukas, Alba University, Athens and Strathclyde University, UK

Professor Tsoukas's work draws on insights from Hayek and others on the essentially distributed nature of knowledge in organisations. Tsoukas rejects the notion that knowledge can be readily taxonomised into discrete categories such as tacit and explicit. Following this argument, all explicit knowledge is dependent on tacit knowledge. Knowledge is inextricably linked to practice. It follows that attempts to centralise knowledge or develop an all-encompassing synoptic view are doomed to failure. As Tsoukas notes:

The key to achieving co-ordinated action does not so much depend on those 'higher-up' collecting more and more knowledge as on those 'lower-down' finding more and more ways of getting connected and interrelating the knowledge each one has.

Conclusions

This chapter has presented the findings of our questionnaire and of the follow-up discussions with experts in the field. The findings are significant in that they document the research currently being conducted into KM, and how researchers view the challenges facing KM. The chapter found that HRM was viewed as being of great importance to KM. However, the survey also suggested that the current research was not predominantly concerned with HRM *per se*. HRM appeared mainly as a secondary or contextual factor.

The chapter moved on to consider research centres that are currently investigating KM. While any such list could never claim to be exhaustive, our account provides, we believe, a fairly robust outline of university-based KM research in the UK. In addition, it offers brief but useful detail on work taking place elsewhere in the world. This part of the chapter illustrated the burgeoning and dynamic nature of the KM field.

The final section of this chapter has reviewed the central features of the work of theorists adjudged, by their peer group of fellow researchers, to be particularly important to the current discourse on KM. The pen-portraits we have presented aim to capture the key tenets of the theorists' work, together with a discussion of the potential implications of their message for HRM.

In our view, this study has made a substantial contribution to mapping the field of KM in terms of the views of researchers, the major themes being investigated and research centres and researchers of particular note. This in itself reflects that KM is maturing as perhaps a 'meta-discipline'. The distinctive feature of this chapter has been to situate KM within the context of HRM concerns.

5 | Analysing the relationship between KM and HRM

◘ **This chapter seeks to elucidate the complex interactions between KM and HRM practices. KM is seen as a wide-ranging set of practices rather than a uniform discipline.**

◘ **Five different perspectives are identified on the relationship between KM, HRM and economic performance: HRM best practice, knowledge workers, congruence of practices, human and social capital and different forms of learning.**

Knowledge management (KM) has been hailed as the critical ingredient of competitive success in the knowledge-based economy. Yet, as previous reports for the CIPD have indicated (Scarbrough *et al*, 1999), much of the existing theory and practice of KM is narrowly focused on the use of IT to communicate and store information. Although IT is an important enabling factor in the development of KM, it is dangerous to assume that new IT systems such as the corporate intranet actually offer a solution to the KM issue. An accumulating body of evidence demonstrates that the actions and perceptions of managers and employees are the most powerful determinant of the success of KM, regardless of the particular IT system employed. While this evidence is certainly a corrective to what might be termed the 'technocratic' approach to KM, it is scattered across a range of different studies whose findings are only now beginning to appear. Some of these studies are directly concerned with KM, but others are only indirectly related, being focused on a range of relevant but tangential subjects such as the pay of knowledge worker groups, the development of trust, the management of innovation, and so on. It follows that in order to assess the whole range of links between HRM and

KM we need to locate this study in a broader context, which encompasses the mediating factors that influence the management of knowledge in organisations.

Scope of KM

One of the problems in seeking to elucidate the links between KM and HRM is the ambitious and wide-ranging nature of the KM agenda. Knowledge is such a protean element of organisational performance that any discussion of managing knowledge quickly branches out into a number of different tasks and issues. It follows that KM is not a uniform management discipline, but encompasses a variety of different terms and practices. Knowledge itself appears in a number of different guises according to context:

◘ 'Intellectual capital' (eg Bontis, 1998; Edvinsson and Malone, 1997; Roos *et al*, 1998; Stewart, 1997; Sullivan, 1998)

◘ 'Knowledge assets' (Boisot, 1998; Teece, 1998)

◘ 'Workplace and organisational learning' (Adler and Cole; 1993; Argyris, 1992; Baum and

> 'Although IT is an important enabling factor in the development of KM, it is dangerous to assume that new IT systems such as the corporate intranet actually offer a solution to the KM issue.'

Ingram, 1997; Dixon, 1994; Easterby-Smith *et al*, 1999; Huber, 1991; March, 1999; Powell *et al*, 1996; Sanchez and Heene, 1997; Senge, 1990).

Likewise, KM practices might encompass a range of different activities, including, for instance, systems that measure and account for intellectual capital; the exploitation of intellectual property rights; and the capture of project-based learning. Although much interesting work is being carried out to address the way knowledge can be more accurately represented and accounted for, the primary focus of this report is on the management rather than the representation of knowledge. In other words, KM will be viewed as the attempt by management to actively create, communicate and exploit knowledge as a resource for the organisation. This attempt has both technical, social and economic components:

- ◘ In technical terms it involves centralising knowledge that is currently scattered across the organisation and codifying tacit forms of knowledge. In this more centralised and explicit form, knowledge can be accessed by a variety of groups according to business needs.

- ◘ In social and political terms, KM involves collectivising knowledge so that it is no longer the exclusive property of individuals or groups. Knowledge is abstracted from highly situated processes of social learning such that its use is no longer so closely tied to its creation.

- ◘ In economic terms, KM is a response to organisations' need to intensify their creation and exploitation of knowledge. This reflects the rising competitive pressures for innovation and the more rapid turnover of new products and services. KM increases the throughput rate for

converting knowledge into new products and services.

It is possible to see a number of different relationships between KM and HRM practices depending on the model of KM that is applied. Clearly, this would militate against any notion of there being an optimal set of HRM practices for the creation and utilisation of knowledge in organisations. At the same time, the co-existence of different approaches to KM with many different patterns of HRM practice highlights the complex nature of their interactions. In the section below, we seek to address this complexity by identifying and outlining some of the ways in which such interactions may operate.

Analysing relationships between KM and HRM

Just as KM has been interpreted and enacted in various ways, it is important to recognise that HRM is equally amenable to a variety of interpretations – both theoretical and practical. It is not within the scope of this report to debate these different interpretations. This is better handled elsewhere (eg Storey, 1989). Although KM has only recently emerged as a specific set of concepts and practices, it is important to recognise that the role of HRM in fostering and exploiting knowledge assets has been a subject of debate for some time. Much of that debate has centred on the management of knowledge workers – a term coined by Peter Drucker. More recently, the concept of the 'learning organisation' has created a good deal of interest in the HRM community, with a number of studies addressing the HRM components of such an organisation. So it would be inaccurate to suggest that little thought has been given to the role of HRM in knowledge-based organisations. However, it is true to say that

> ' ... there is ... a good deal of evidence to suggest that the effect of different HRM practices is context-specific – that the same practices may have different effects or be interpreted differently in one organisation compared to another.'

hitherto the emergence of a literature on KM practice has not been matched by a corresponding interest in its HRM implications. As noted earlier, many of the studies addressing KM are primarily concerned with the use of IT rather than with HRM issues. Where HRM practices are mentioned in such accounts, it is often in fairly superficial terms, stressing the need, for example, to ensure employee commitment or a 'supportive culture' if KM is to be successful (Quinn *et al*, 1996).

Despite this lack of attention hitherto, it is possible to identify some studies that have tentatively begun to sketch out the lineaments of an HRM contribution to the practice of KM. These studies help to provide a road-map for our analysis of relevant research by indicating a number of different perspectives on the relationship between HRM and KM. As we noted in Chapter 3, the impact of HRM practices on performance can be understood in a number of different ways. Making these different understandings explicit is an important step towards a more judicious application of HRM policy and practice to the management of knowledge.

From the existing literature, then, it is possible to identify five major perspectives on the interactions between HRM and KM. We have termed them here: HRM best practice; knowledge work; congruence; human and social capital; and learning-based perspectives.

Best practice perspective

Perhaps the most straightforward assessment of the relationship between KM and HRM is the argument that this is best secured by following a best practice recipe for HRM. Mabey *et al* (1998), for example, cite Nonaka and Takeuchi's (1995) work as an example of this argument, especially

the claim that knowledge creation 'is a highly individual process of personal and organisational self-renewal. The personal commitment of employees and their identity with the company and its mission become indispensable.' The particular label attached to best practice varies from one authority to another. 'Business excellence' was the influential aspiration of Peters and Waterman (1982), but more recent candidates include 'strategic human resource management' (Fombrun *et al*, 1984) and 'high commitment management'. Wood (1995), for example, concludes a recent study with the claim: 'The implication of this research is that high commitment management is universally applicable' (p57). Clearly, if the best practice perspective is taken at face value, managers need hardly worry about tailoring their HRM practices to the specific demands of KM initiatives. By following a best practice model they will ensure the level of commitment and capability to encourage knowledge-sharing that will make KM successful. Moreover, this should apply to any organisation, whatever its particular features and circumstances.

Though attractive, however, this argument still leaves one or two questions outstanding. First, even if we accept this view, managers are left with the question of which best practice model to follow, for there are many recipes available. Second, there is also a good deal of evidence to suggest that the effect of different HRM practices is context-specific – that the same practices may have different effects or be interpreted differently in one organisation compared to another (Tyson and Fell, 1986; Collinson *et al*, 1998). And even if the effects were uniform or predictable, the influence of the historical context and management capabilities may prevent the best practice being adopted (Mueller, 1994). This analysis suggests that creating an effective link between HRM practices and KM may involve going beyond best practice to more customised approaches.

Knowledge work perspective

One such approach can be seen in those studies which seek to link HRM practices to the characteristics of knowledge work and knowledge workers. While technologies quickly become obsolete, the skills of knowledge workers are important for a number of reasons (Reich, 1991):

◘ their knowledge and skills are a directly productive force for the company

◘ they represent an investment for the company and not just labour costs

◘ they bring labour-saving benefits in their ability to reorganise production and design

◘ their knowledge represents a form of personal 'equity', and many knowledge workers are potential entrepreneurs.

Knowledge workers are frequently distinguished from more conventional professional groups. Where professionals work *from* knowledge, drawing on a distinctive occupationally defined body of expertise, knowledge workers work *with* knowledge. This includes not only their own expertise but also that of other knowledge workers as communicated through information systems and artefacts, as well as the organisational and technical knowledge encoded in programs, routines and managerial discourse (Scarbrough, 1999). Similarly, Whalley and Orr (1997) analyse knowledge work in terms of the dual processes of 'transformation' and 'maintenance' – knowledge workers transform the objects of their work into

symbolic form, but also maintain the systems and tools they employ.

These characteristics have a number of possible implications for HRM. Given knowledge workers' importance and high salary costs, selection will be more intensive, and there will be greater emphasis on finding the right fit between the individual and other members of the knowledge worker group. Also, training and development can be seen as an investment and not just a cost, because the knowledge workers' expertise is producing direct benefits for the organisation. For these reasons, the rewards offered are higher than for other non-managerial groups. As well as high, performance-related salaries these highly valued employees are often offered a direct stake in the organisation – through stock options, for example – as a means of retaining their skills.

A number of studies have sought to address the implications of knowledge work for HRM practices. One area that has received particular attention is the task of aligning reward systems with the motivational characteristics of knowledge workers. Where other employees may adopt an instrumental attitude to their work – ie focusing on pay – knowledge workers are likely to have wider expectations. Not only is the work itself of greater intrinsic interest to them, but they are also likely to see their job as just one step in a longer-term career – the pay and benefits they get from their current job may be less important than the career benefits of experience and development. Also, managers need to recognise that knowledge workers are interested in both the tangible and intangible rewards of their work. Intangible rewards may include status, reputation and recognition by one's peer group.

A study by Tampoe (1993) identified four key motivators for knowledge workers:

1   Personal growth: the opportunity for individuals to fully realise their potential.

2   Operational autonomy: a work environment in which knowledge workers can achieve the tasks assigned to them. This is more important than the strategic autonomy to actually determine such tasks (Bailyn, 1988).

3   Task achievement: a sense of accomplishment from producing work that is of high quality and relevance to the organisation.

4   Money rewards: an income that is a just reward for their contribution to corporate success and that symbolises their contribution to that success.

Tampoe argues that this motivational set demands greater attention to the individual needs of knowledge workers. He suggests that HRM policies for knowledge workers should concentrate upon achieving:

◘   regular appraisals and career discussions with staff so that their career stages and motivations are fully understood

◘   a supportive working environment in which employees can achieve their preferred motivators, and both tangible and intangible rewards.

These practices seek to ensure that corporate HRM policies are not applied in a blanket way to knowledge worker groups. Although knowledge workers may have some common characteristics, their career needs and motivation will be unique to each individual. In return for high levels of performance, they typically expect to receive more personalised attention from management.

Other, more critical accounts of the management of knowledge workers have stressed the importance of organisational culture and attendant social identities in influencing their motivation and behaviour (Alvesson, 1993). Culture, for example, is seen as playing a socially integrative function for employees whose work is otherwise highly autonomous and individualised (Kunda, 1992). Likewise, the social identities that knowledge workers develop through their work are seen as playing a critical role in motivation, and even their willingness to join and stay with a particular firm.

This view of the distinctive characteristics of knowledge workers suggests that the implications for organisations extend beyond HRM practices alone – though these are seen as critical – to the whole management process. A recent study of Microsoft provides some insights into this wider impact and its importance for business success (Cusumano and Selby, 1996). In this account, Microsoft's success reflects the way in which the company has developed a distinctive culture and structure that avoids the usual clash of values and practices between management and knowledge workers. This involves ensuring that management practice is grounded four-square on both knowledge of technology and knowledge of the business. The company possesses a 'CEO with a deep understanding of both the technology and the business' (p23) and 'managers who both create the product and make the technical decisions' (p26). It ensures that managers retain their technical expertise by continuing to work part time as developers. Similarly, bureaucratic over-control is avoided through process design and cultural features. For example, Microsoft have put in place a development process that 'allows large teams to work like small teams' (p25). The prevailing culture is also seen to play an important

> '**Traditionally, knowledge workers have enjoyed a good
> deal of autonomy and have not been managed as tightly
> as other groups.**'

role. Shared values and high levels of employee commitment allow management to accept a high degree of employee autonomy and yet still achieve the necessary degree of control over product development.

Finally, individual needs are also addressed in the Microsoft organisation. This happens, first, through an intensive process of self-selection, which ensures a good fit between the individual and the organisation. Second, Microsoft reduce the conflict between individual self-interest and organisational goals by integrating individual expertise within a collective framework. This they do, for example, by ensuring that knowledge of product development details is possessed by more than one person, thus avoiding the creation of 'prima donnas'. Product development is controlled by program managers rather than individual 'superprogrammers' for the same reason. At the same time, high-performing employees are rewarded with stock options, which gives them a tangible stake in the company's future performance.

The success of firms such as Microsoft has highlighted the critical importance of the management process for this group. Traditionally, knowledge workers have enjoyed a good deal of autonomy and have not been managed as tightly as other groups. They have posed problems for the application of concepts such as business process re-engineering, for example. Davenport *et al* (1996) acknowledge the limitations of conventional process improvement approaches for knowledge work. They suggest that these limitations derive from two sources:

1   The nature of the work itself: knowledge work cannot be as readily prescribed as operational or administrative work since there will always

be an element of intuition involved in the creative application of expertise.

2   The nature of knowledge workers: the training and education of knowledge workers has led them to expect some autonomy in their work. They expect to be able to use their professional and technical judgement and expertise, rather than simply follow a prescribed routine.

Given these factors, Davenport *et al* argue that a new approach is needed. Specifically, they suggest it is possible to identify three different strategies to improve the work processes involved in knowledge work:

1   Change the unit of knowledge so that knowledge has a more modular quality, making it easier to slot together in different ways.

2   Change where and with whom people work so that knowledge can be combined in different ways and more easily.

3   Employ technological enablers so that individuals can more easily share their knowledge with others, even when working in geographically separated locations.

These attempts to move away from *laissez-faire* approaches and to integrate the management of knowledge workers much more closely into streamlined business processes is symptomatic of what is likely to be an increasing drive to secure greater efficiency and value added from this increasingly important group.

Congruence perspective

This perspective can be seen as a development of the knowledge work perspective in that it similarly seeks to adapt HRM practices to contingent circumstances, except that here the aim is the more ambitious one of extending the account beyond knowledge-intensive firms to organisations in general.

One of the most influential recent contributions to this perspective comes from Hansen, Nohria and Tierney (1999). Though not specifically concerned with HRM, but with 'knowledge management strategy', this article does identify some important relationships between HRM and KM. Hansen *et al* argue that there are basically two KM strategies: 'codification' and 'personalisation'.

◨ Codification: 'Knowledge is carefully codified and stored in databases where it can be accessed and used readily by anyone in the company' (p107).

◨ Personalisation: 'Knowledge is closely tied to the person who developed it and is shared mainly through direct person-to-person contacts' (p107).

These strategies drive the management practices of the organisation as outlined in Table 2.

This analysis does not claim that organisations pursue these strategies exclusively – firms with a codification strategy also engage in personalisation to some degree. However, Hansen *et al* argue that competitive success involves pursuing one strategy predominantly. Success comes from an 80–20 split in strategic emphasis. Failure comes from attempting to 'straddle' both strategies equally.

The analysis presented here is open to criticism, of course. For one, the account of personalisation emphasises the role of individual experts but glosses over the importance of groups and

Table 2 | Knowledge management strategies

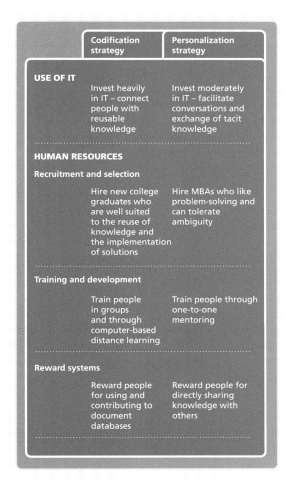

	Codification strategy	Personalization strategy
USE OF IT	Invest heavily in IT – connect people with reusable knowledge	Invest moderately in IT – facilitate conversations and exchange of tacit knowledge
HUMAN RESOURCES		
Recruitment and selection	Hire new college graduates who are well suited to the reuse of knowledge and the implementation of solutions	Hire MBAs who like problem-solving and can tolerate ambiguity
Training and development	Train people in groups and through computer-based distance learning	Train people through one-to-one mentoring
Reward systems	Reward people for using and contributing to document databases	Reward people for directly sharing knowledge with others

communities in creating and sharing knowledge. This may be valid for consultancy firms that employ highly talented individuals, but it is debatable whether it applies to all organisations in the way that Hansen *et al* claim. Also, the argument that organisations must pursue one predominant KM strategy is plausible – echoing Porter's (1980) influential analysis of competitive advantage as the result of either cost reduction or differentiation. But, it is based on limited empirical evidence and is subject to the same criticisms that have been directed at Porter's work.

As far as HRM is concerned, however, the Hansen *et al* account makes several useful contributions. First, it links both KM and HRM to the competitive strategy of the organisation. This is a useful corrective to the many articles that imply that KM is all about creating massive IT databases – as if the sheer quantity of 'knowledge' communicated and stored was the secret of business success. Hansen *et al* show that it is not knowledge *per se* but the way it is applied to strategic objectives that is the critical ingredient of competitiveness. Second, this account effectively demonstrates the need to adapt HRM practices to the KM strategy in use. As the authors note:

The two knowledge management strategies call for different incentive systems. In the codification model, managers need to develop a system that encourages people to write down what they know and to get those documents into the electronic repository … companies that are following the personalization approach … need to reward people for sharing knowledge directly with other people … (p113).

As reflected in the quote above, the Hansen *et al* article is arguing in effect for what can be termed a 'congruence' perspective on the relationship between KM and HRM. They claim that KM strategies require a strong internal and external 'fit' (Fombrun *et al*,1984) between management practices and the business environment, such that HRM practices need to be contingent on the use of IT, KM practices and overall competitive strategy. In this perspective, HRM policies and practices need to be internally consistent – ie they all need to be pulling in the same direction. At the same time such practices need to be aligned with the overall management system in the organisation. It is this systemic interaction between different functional areas that enhances performance. Management practices in each area are mutually reinforcing such that the overall effect is greater than the sum of the parts.

This emphasis on the systemic role of HRM finds echoes in other accounts of competitiveness. In his study of lean production, for example, MacDuffie (1995) finds strong evidence to suggest that the alignment of 'bundles' of HRM policies – linking reward, training and employee involvement – with the demands of lean production systems can significantly enhance competitiveness.

Human and social capital perspective

The congruence perspective on the role of HRM finds support from a number of quarters (eg Tyson, 1995). However, it is not the only possible perspective on this relationship. Other studies of the role of knowledge in organisational performance tend to suggest an alternative account. This differs from the congruence perspective on a number of counts. First, the congruence perspective is essentially *managerial* in its focus. The rational adaptation of management practice is seen as the key to success. The behaviour and perceptions of those who are being managed is secondary. In contrast, other views of

'... the primary contribution of HRM is the long-term development of skills, culture and capabilities within the organisation.'

the role of knowledge emphasise the essentially *social* nature of organisations. Thus the firm is viewed as a social institution (Kogut and Zander, 1992) whose aims are achieved primarily through the social resources and relationships it creates in the pursuit of economic goals. In this view, the effect of HRM practice is defined not so much by its short-term alignment with other management functions as by its long-term implications for the development of human resources and relationships. In other words, the primary contribution of HRM is the long-term development of skills, culture and capabilities within the organisation (Stalk *et al*, 1992).

Second, this view of the influence of HRM draws attention to a different aspect of knowledge management. The Hansen *et al* account stresses the *flows* of knowledge within the organisation – from people to people, or from people to IT systems. However, as Starbuck (1992) points out, *stocks* of knowledge are equally important. Stocks take a number of forms, including informal routines and individual and group expertise, together with the knowledge encoded in computer systems and organisational procedures. These stocks accumulate from what Starbuck terms the firm's input-output systems, such as hiring, training and the purchase of capital goods. Stocks develop from the inflows of R&D and the development of culture. They are depleted through turnover, imitated routines and sales of capital goods.

Stocks of knowledge have been popularly represented in the literature on KM as different contributions to the intellectual capital of the organisation (Edvinsson and Malone, 1997; Stewart, 1997; Sveiby, 1997) – as represented, for instance, in Figure 2:

These different forms of 'capital' draw attention to the capabilities of the organisation and the way they evolve over time. These terms are briefly described below (Gordon and Ives, 1997).

Figure 2 | The formation of intellectual capital

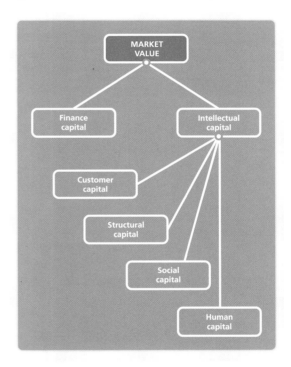

Financial capital

The financial assets of the organisation: appropriate metrics include the traditional performance measures that would be used to determine whether the overall investments in information systems, training and education, etc. are increasing the revenue generated per employee.

Customer capital

The quality of the organisation's relationship with its customers: broadly measured in terms of customer retention and satisfaction, but also includes factors such as year-on-year growth of new customers versus current customers; number of products or services considered to be the best in the world; and measures of the employees' knowledge of the customer.

Structural capital

This is said to include everything that remains when knowledge workers go home: the physical assets that affect the organisation's capability to effectively create and produce knowledge. Structural capital includes areas such as work environment, information systems, databases, workgroup tools for collaboration, organisational structures and business processes. Examples of performance metrics to support structural capital measures include the percentage of processes that are world class as defined by industry standards; number of processes documented; and even the percentage of employees equipped with portable laptops and Internet access.

Human capital

The value employees bring to the organisation, encompassing the whole range of human abilities and potential. This means individual expertise certainly, but also commitment and creativity. Here measures are more difficult and context-specific, but progress in accounting for 'intangible assets' is beginning to make the contribution of human capital more visible.

Social capital

This has been defined as 'networks of relationships (that) constitute a valuable resource for the conduct of social affairs' (Nahapiet and Ghoshal, 1998, p243). Social capital makes an important contribution to the development and exploitation of intellectual capital. Much of the knowledge created by individuals and teams is socially embedded – ie it can be accessed and exploited only through participation in 'communities of practice' (Lave and Wenger, 1991). Development of social capital, for example through the cultivation of such communities, promotes greater knowledge-sharing and therefore more intensive and efficient exploitation of knowledge for organisational goals.

The human and social capital perspective on the relationship between HRM and KM draws attention to the impact of HRM practices on the accumulation of stocks of knowledge within the organisation. In this perspective, HRM makes its contribution to business strategy not so much by seeking a fit with the overall management approach as by shaping what have been termed the 'core competencies' (Prahalad and Hamel, 1990) of the organisation. This places the effect of HRM practices squarely in the territory of the 'resource-based theory of the firm'. As noted earlier in our account of Robert Grant's work, this view emphasises that firms compete not through their short-term positioning in markets – the Porter (1980) orthodoxy – but through the long-run development of unique and inimitable resources. It

'The success or failure of KM, it seems, may depend not so much on the character of current HRM practices as on the consequences of HRM actions five, 10 or even 20 years ago.'

is particularly relevant to the discussion of different forms of intellectual capital because these are highly inimitable resources, which are shaped to a large extent through the organisation's own evolution – they are core resources.

Proponents of this perspective on the contribution of HRM practices see it as rescuing such practices from long-term neglect: Thus Prahalad and Hamel (1990) comment:

We find it ironic that top management devotes so much attention to the capital budgeting process yet typically has no comparable mechanism for allocating the human skills that embody 'core competencies (p87).

Capelli and Singh (1992) are enthusiastic about the implications of the resource-based view. They see such implications principally in terms of the role that HRM practices play in creating distinctive competencies for firms. They argue, for instance, that HRM policies offer important means of capturing distinctive human resources and then of developing those resources internally to create inimitable assets. The policies they recommend include measures to ensure the retention of valued employees, including 'backloaded' reward systems. They also recommend the creation of firm-specific skills, both directly through internal training programmes and indirectly through employment security.

For Capelli and Singh, these moves demonstrate the possibilities opened up by a new relationship between HRM and business strategy. Instead of asking 'how management decisions, typically at the business-strategy level affect labour relations outcomes' (p186), they pose a new question: 'How employment practices … affect competitive advantage and, ultimately, business strategy' (p186). Hewlett-Packard, they claim, 'avoids

proprietary contracts because the fluctuations in production entailed in such work would disrupt the job security and internal labour market programs' (p186).

Overall, the implication of this perspective is to highlight the long-term effects of HRM practices – on employee relations, culture and levels of trust – over their more formal characteristics. One consequence is to caution against the idea that congruence alone – all functions 'singing from the same hymn-sheet' – is the key to an effective relationship between HRM and KM. The success or failure of KM, it seems, may depend not so much on the character of current HRM practices as on the consequences of HRM actions five, 10 or even 20 years ago. For these are the timescales over which the critical ingredients of intellectual capital are formed.

This does not necessarily lead to a fatalistic view of the prospects for KM, though it might help to explain why even the most brilliantly managed KM initiatives sometimes fail. It does, however, suggest that HRM practices need to be evaluated more precisely in relation to their impact on the sources of intellectual capital. In particular, we need to explore their impact on human capital and social capital respectively.

Impact of HRM on human capital

Human capital is something that individual employees bring to the organisation, but which is also developed through experience and training within the organisation. It is clearly vital to the success of KM since much of the knowledge – especially tacit knowledge – that it mobilises is embodied in individuals. On the other hand, the integrity of human capital as a knowledge asset is precarious. This is because the potential mobility of individual employees undermines the firm's ability to appropriate the skills they bring to the organisation. Studies of professional service firms depending heavily on individuals (Alvesson, 1995) provide many examples of the fragility of the competitive advantage based on individual experts. The acquisition of the firm itself may count for nothing if its major assets are able to leave and set up in business elsewhere.

This appropriability problem can be addressed to some extent by ensuring that individual capacities are organisationally embedded in the form of corporate routines and collective skills. This depends, however, as Grant observes, on the power relationship between employer and employee:

The degree of control exercised by a firm and the balance of power between the firm and an individual employee depends crucially on the relationship between the individual's skills and organisational routines. The more deeply embedded are organisational routines within groups of individuals and the more they are supported by the contributions of other resources, then the greater is the control that the firm's management can exercise

(Grant, 1991, p128).

Thus, Grant distinguishes between 'brilliant individuals' and 'team assets', with only the latter offering significant competitive advantage.

This account highlights the value of a concern with human capital, especially in knowledge-intensive settings where the work is individualised and performance depends on individual skills and motivation. On the other hand, even in knowledge-intensive settings, research (eg Keegan, 1998) shows that social relations are crucial to high performance. Knowledge workers are particularly concerned with their social identity at work, and this may be just as important as material rewards. Also, in some contexts, knowledge may be the product of collective and team-based learning (eg teams in R&D labs or in production areas) (Kamoche and Mueller, 1998).

Impact of HRM on social capital

The impact of HRM practices on social capital is likely to be greatest in the following areas:

Social identity: selection processes, career development and performance management systems exert an important influence on the identities forged by individuals within an organisation – eg highly rigorous selection may create a strong élite identity among particular groups, which is reinforced by highly leveraged reward systems. Shared identities enhance employees' willingness to share knowledge (Lewicki and Bunker, 1996).

Trust: an integral element of social capital is the trust that emerges through reliable interactions between groups and individuals. Although trust is sometimes presented as an amorphous ingredient of good management, the range of different forms of trust and the different processes through which they are formed highlights the need to understand the social interactions involved at a more detailed level. Again, a number of HRM practices may affect the development of trust. Reward systems that focus on individual performance, for example, are often seen as undermining interpersonal trust, though they may equally increase trust between managers and employees through the transparency of their operation.

Teamworking: this is sometimes presented in narrowly functional terms as a more flexible division of labour, but it also depends upon and advances social capital in organisations. Team-based knowledge may not be amenable to codification but may be exploitable through the development of strong team and inter-team relationships. HRM practices again affect the development of team-working at a number of levels, including the design of work organisation, reward systems and patterns of employee relations.

Social networks: the role of networks in knowledge management is increasingly recognised through research studies (eg Hansen, 1999) that demonstrate that the configuration of such networks – eg strong ties versus weak ties – is important in influencing the kinds of knowledge that can be exchanged between groups and individuals. This is partly to do with the improved ease of access to knowledge, but also reflects the extent to which valuable knowledge is often controlled by specific groups or individuals – in other words, who you know affects what you know. The benefits of social networks may also be transferable from one setting to another, and thus may facilitate the development of innovations and new activities.

These different manifestations of social capital help to demonstrate its implications for competitive performance. They represent important mediating influences on the success of KM initiatives. At the same time, they incorporate the effects of managerial strategies and policies over a long-term period. In particular, they reflect the cumulative consequences of HRM practice over that period; not, perhaps, the fine detail of such practice, but certainly its broad patterning of social

relations through the interactions between selection processes, career paths, development opportunities and performance management systems.

Tyson (1995) highlights some of these HRM-influenced patterns in organisational evolution when he contrasts the impact of 'hard' versus 'soft' contracting as keynotes of HRM policy (see Table 3).

Table 3 | Hard versus soft contracting in HRM policy

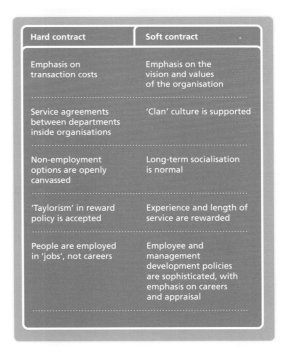

Hard contract	Soft contract
Emphasis on transaction costs	Emphasis on the vision and values of the organisation
Service agreements between departments inside organisations	'Clan' culture is supported
Non-employment options are openly canvassed	Long-term socialisation is normal
'Taylorism' in reward policy is accepted	Experience and length of service are rewarded
People are employed in 'jobs', not careers	Employee and management development policies are sophisticated, with emphasis on careers and appraisal

Clearly, the hard contracting approach views the organisation as an instrument for the co-ordination of economic activities, whereas soft contracting highlights its institutional role in the integration of social units. The former seeks to replicate market relations while the latter is explicitly managed – involving an elaborate internal labour market and a sophisticated HRM function. These different types or, better, dimensions of HRM policy – for no firm matches this model entirely – are well-known patterns of firm evolution. Much of the attention until now, however, has focused on their different consequences for relations between employees and management. The concept of social capital, however, draws attention much more explicitly to their effects on relations between employee groups themselves. The soft contracting mode involves a long-term process of socialisation through developed career paths. Here deep social affiliations and communities of practice are much more likely to flourish than in the harsh, short-term environment of hard contracting. The result is that not only is the organisation potentially more flexible in dealing with the transactional uncertainties of change and innovation, but – an equally important consideration – it is likely to enjoy greater capabilities in these areas because of its endowment of socially embedded skills and knowledge.

This is not to say that soft contracting represents the best option in every circumstance. Firms that are subject to extreme competitive pressures may find that hard contracting is the only feasible option available to them. It is also fair to note that the embeddedness (Granovetter, 1985) of social relations may sometimes prove to be an obstacle to change. Deeply embedded communities, such as long-established professional groupings, may prove to be centres of resistance under certain circumstances. As Nahapiet and Ghoshal acknowledge: 'organisations high in social capital may become ossified through their relatively restricted access to diverse sources of ideas and information' (1998, p260). Where change is extremely rapid and discontinuous – the Schumpeterian model of creative destruction – firms with no baggage of history or developed social ties may enjoy a temporary advantage. On the other hand, eventually even the newest and smallest firms may find that their survival is as much a result of their preciously acquired social capital – family ties, or loyalty to the team or the owner – as the hard-nosed business decisions of their managers (Whittington, 1988; Scarbrough, 2000).

Overall, the broad characterisation of hard and soft contracting helps us to grasp some of the specific mechanisms through which HRM policies can help or hinder the development of social capital in organisations. Policies that are narrowly economic in focus and which view employees as a disposable commodity are broadly antithetical to developing and sustaining human and social capital. Policies that view the organisation as a social institution, stressing socialisation, integration and development, seem on current evidence more likely to generate the endogenous capabilities that underpin long-term competitive success.

Learning perspective

The relationship between knowledge and learning is both intimate and interdependent. Many writers (eg Boisot, 1998) view knowledge as the product of social learning processes of various kinds. Under this perspective we have grouped those studies that see the links between KM and HRM essentially in terms of the creation or management of learning processes. There are many different strands to this perspective as learning takes place on a number of different levels, including individual, group and organisational learning. The major interest in terms of HRM, however, is defined by two groups of studies – those dealing with organisational and community learning, respectively.

Organisational learning

One of the most important concepts in this field is the notion of the learning organisation (LO). This has become an influential movement in which HRM practices and practitioners take a leading role. The LO has been defined as an organisation that is able to discover what is effective by reframing its own experiences and learning from that process. Proponents distinguish between the LO and the more nebulous concept of organisational learning. Learning occurs in various guises in all organisations, but not all organisations are learning organisations.

This movement owes much its impact to the success of Peter Senge's (1990) book, *The Fifth Discipline: The art and practice of the learning organisation*. According to Senge, an LO is:

… where people continually expand their capacity to create the results they truly desire, where new and expansive patterns of thinking are nurtured, where collective aspiration is set free, and where people are continually learning how to learn together (1990, p4).

There is a strong emphasis on creating the conditions in which individual and collective creativity may flourish, with the management of

people – ie their values, attitudes, collective beliefs, languages and discourses – being at the core of any LO initiative. Training and development and human resource practices are central since an LO continuously transforms itself by developing the skills of all its people (Pedler, Burgoyne and Boydell, 1991). Senge's work – which percolates through many of the other studies in this field – is based on a systems theory of organisations. From this standpoint, he identifies five disciplines which, he claims, are necessary for becoming an LO. These are: personal mastery, mental models, shared vision, team learning, and systems thinking.

As noted earlier, the LO is only one of the available strands on learning. The latter field is increasingly divergent, and there is an extensive literature on 'organisational learning' that is both more broadly based and arguably more conceptually rigorous than LO texts (Easterby-Smith *et al*, 1998). In this literature, the philosophy of the LO is criticised for failing to address the unique contextual factors influencing learning processes. An important theme is to see organisational learning as embedded in a wider institutional context of interorganisational relationships (Geppert, 1996).

Although both the LO and organisational learning studies offer some important insights into the way in which knowledge and learning are fostered by management practice, they have been overshadowed, at least in terms of practitioner interest, by the explosive growth of activity in the area of KM (Scarbrough *et al*, 1999). This may be attributable to the problems of translating their broad, holistic principles into practice. KM initiatives, by contrast, are often more specifically targeted and can therefore be identified more closely with business needs. The organisation-level focus has often been sidelined in such studies.

> ' 'Communities of practice' … are seen as important because it is within such communities that much of the organisation's tacit knowledge is created and shared.'

Community learning

One strand of the learning perspective that has been influential in the KM field, however, is that group of studies that have focused not on the organisation as a whole but on specific groups within it. 'Communities of practice' are groups of people who may be distributed across an organisation but who share a common dedication to specific work practices. They are seen as important because it is within such communities that much of the organisation's tacit knowledge is created and shared. This view challenges the assumption that knowledge is primarily a cognitive phenomenon, but argues that knowledge is inherently social in nature (Collins, 1990) – ie it emerges from the collective experience of work and is shared and communicated between members of a particular group or community (Lave and Wenger, 1991). In this account, forms of knowledge are more or less tacit or explicit in relation to a particular community, and their exploitation is dependent on the practices of that community. Story-telling as a way of communicating knowledge is more important than codifying it in IT systems (Brown and Duguid, 1991).

At first glance, the 'community of practice' view of learning may seem rather nebulous. The term 'community of practice' does not appear on any organisation chart. Nor does it feature in the different business processes designed by management. As Brown and Duguid (1998) note: 'communities of practice do not necessarily think of themselves as a community in the conventional sense. Equally, conventional communities are not necessarily communities of practice' (p96). We also need to distinguish between teams and communities of practice. Teams are created for specific projects, and team members are selected by management for their ability to contribute to that project. The team disbands when the project is completed. In contrast, communities of practice are not time bounded or dedicated to a specific project. Becoming a member is usually an informal and self-selecting process, though some organisations are now beginning to formalise community membership. Communities of practice also pose a challenge to traditional management approaches. Attempts to create communities of practice in a top-down way often fail because these groups depend on bottom-up involvement and commitment to be successful.

Yet, while they may be hard to identify and manage, communities of practice may play a crucial role in sharing knowledge across the organisation. A good example of this is provided by Orr's (1990) study of customer service representatives who repair the photocopiers of Xerox customers. Orr established that in informal meetings with other reps over breakfast, lunch and coffee, this group would continuously swap war stories about malfunctioning machines that could not be repaired simply by going through the know-what of the repair manual. Orr found that one of these informal conversations would be worth hours of training. The importance of the community of practice in sharing knowledge and learning is supported by Brown and Duguid (1998). They make a distinction between 'know-what' and 'know-how', arguing that know-how includes the ability to put know-what into practice and is typically found among work groups engaged co-operatively in the same work practices.

The community approach obviously has great relevance to the relationship between KM and HRM. The implications of HRM for the development of such communities is described in more detail above when we dealt with the issue of social capital. There are some caveats attaching to this approach, however. In particular, viewing the organisation as a mosaic of different communities may tend to impute greater harmony and unity to the organisation than exists in reality. This may not only play down the problems of inter-group conflict, but may also neglect some of the tensions that exist between individuals and the organisation. Such tensions may well limit the organisation's ability to 'appropriate' the learning developed by individuals and groups (Kamoche and Mueller, 1998). It follows that as well as cultivating and fostering communities of practice, managers also need to be mindful of mechanisms,

such as teamworking, for example, through which individual and group learning can be translated into an organisational resource.

Conclusions

This is necessarily an abbreviated account of the many possible perspectives that could be brought to bear on the relationship between KM and HRM. In identifying five major perspectives on that relationship, we have aimed to provide the reader with a useful, if not very detailed, road-map of the burgeoning research activity in this area. Although drawing on different literatures, theories and value positions, overall the perspectives outlined here do help us to understand the many different ways in which HRM practices may impact on the success of KM – see Figure 3.

Figure 3 | Factors mediating the relationship between KM and HRM

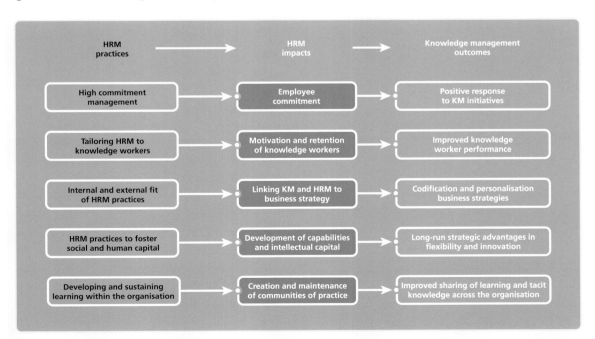

6 | Conclusions

◪   **This chapter reflects on the lessons learnt from this study of the contribution of HRM to KM. It highlights the growing awareness of the saliency of HRM practices in influencing the effectiveness of KM initiatives.**

◪   **Much research and analysis is still at the stage of viewing HRM practices as hygiene factors – ie potential causes of dissatisfaction, but not drivers of success.**

◪   **Developing a positive HRM agenda for the management of knowledge involves focusing on three critical arenas in which HRM practices may influence the creation and exploitation of knowledge: policy, resources and context.**

◪   **Analysing the interaction between HRM and KM in these terms generates a more focused research and policy agenda for the future development of HRM practices.**

It would obviously be inappropriate to attempt to synthesise or summarise the account we have provided here of the extensive and diverse array of research activities relevant to the links between HRM and KM. What our survey demonstrates unequivocally is that the emergence of KM has generated a great amount of research, much of which, given the timescales of such activity, is still in process. For research at this stage we can only describe intentions, not outcomes, and it seems likely that many of the issues we have raised in this report will be more fully addressed when some of these projects publish their findings. Significantly, however, of the researchers who responded to our sample, a large percentage reported that they could identify HRM implications from their work. This provides further positive support for the arguments of a second-generation, more people-centred approach to KM.

In terms of CIPD-sponsored research, again we need to reserve judgement on what are likely to be some of the most important contributions to this

debate; the most relevant projects, notably those led by Professors Purcell and Guest, are still at a relatively early stage. Available outputs from other CIPD studies, however, do at least provide strong support for the contention that HRM practices exert a powerful influence on business performance. This finding contributes to the present debate in two ways. First, it underlines the practical need to integrate KM programmes with HRM policy and practice if ultimate performance is to be enhanced and not impaired. Second, the study of the 'bundling' of HRM practices, though still a matter of contention, does raise important parallels with the implementation of KM. Such parallels would suggest that management practices do not operate in isolation – that they are mutually reinforcing – and that effectiveness derives from the interlinking of such practices. Thus KM systems and practices not only need to be consistent with each other, but also with the wider array of management practices, including, and we would argue especially, HRM. Indeed, this point is further affirmed, as we noted in the

> **'While much of this report has concentrated on the contribution of HRM to KM, it is equally important to recognise that HRM policies have their own limitations.'**

previous chapter, by work on 'congruence' between KM and HRM practices.

Overall, therefore, taking account of both ongoing KM research and the work sponsored by the CIPD, we seem to be arriving at a more optimistic assessment of the developing research and policy agenda. Some of the more vaporous outpourings of technology-driven KM – the notions of 'stockpiling' knowledge and massive knowledge databases – seem to be dispersing in favour of a more pragmatic, and hopefully more holistic engagement with organisational realities. This may provide a conducive context for revising KM theory and practice, incorporating some of the important mediating factors discussed in Chapter 5: employee commitment, communities of practice, human and social capital, and so on.

On the other hand, there is always the danger, as with any HRM development, of token rather than substantive change: that increased recognition of the importance of 'human factors' may translate only into lip-service and not practical action. As we noted earlier of our survey responses, the numbers who acknowledge potential HRM implications are far greater than those who place HRM concerns at the centre of their work. As we observed also in our review of the existing literature, there is a tendency for writers and practitioners to invoke HRM factors to explain the gap between the rhetoric and reality of particular initiatives. Behavioural problems around 'culture', 'resistance', 'attitudes to knowledge-sharing', and so on (eg Quinn *et al*, 1996; Pan and Scarbrough, 1998) are frequently cited in the literature. This association of behavioural issues with KM failure suggests that HRM practices may be being cited as a 'hygiene factor' in some organisations – ie something that can cause dissatisfaction but which is not a driver of success.

If there is a danger of HRM practices being cited in a tokenistic way around KM initiatives, an equally worrying possibility would be managers overstating their effects. While much of this report has concentrated on the contribution of HRM to KM, it is equally important to recognise that HRM policies have their own limitations. They can influence but not command crucial mediating factors such as desired behavioural responses from employees, or the stock of human and social capital available to the firm. In particular, managers need to recognise the temporal aspects of HRM interventions. For example, a culture that is resistant to the development of KM is the product of an organisation's long-term evolution. It cannot be changed except palliatively by the short-term ministrations of a shift in HRM policy. Attempts to use HRM practices to solve the social and cultural problems created by a 'technical fix' are likely to founder on this mismatch between the time horizons of the problem and the putative solution.

Towards an agenda for research

The cumulative effect of the points noted above is to direct our attention away from the idea that HRM can be readily invoked to support particular KM initiatives. Given the different timescales of cause and effect noted above, the bolt-on effectiveness of HRM policy must be limited. Rather, to avoid tokenism we need to reflect on the perspectives on the influence of HRM outlined in Chapter 5, and seek to differentiate more carefully both the possible impacts and time-horizons of HRM practices in relation to the behaviours and resources that sustain the management of knowledge in organisations. Such differentiation suggests three major arenas of HRM influence on knowledge-creation and deployment. These can broadly be termed: policy, resources and context. The following paragraphs summarise each of these arenas in turn and outline their interaction with KM.

Policy

In reviewing the 'congruence' perspective on KM and HRM, we noted the importance of aligning HRM policies both with each other and with the wider business strategy. This was seen as mutually reinforcing and associated with high performance. The need for alignment could also be applied at an operational level to the distinctive characteristics of knowledge worker groups – the need to tailor reward and development policies to their particular needs.

Policies can be changed in the short term and have an immediate impact on the formal specification of management practices. However, they also have medium- and long-term consequences in terms of resources and context.

Resources

A key contribution of HRM, noted particularly in relation to knowledge workers, was the acquisition and retention of valued employees. The importance of managing the employment relationship such that it generates resources for the organisation obviously links to the recruitment and retention of staff. Management practices create human resources from the flow of staff through the organisation. Rewards systems, career paths and mechanisms such as team-working and quality improvement initiatives all serve to draw out and develop employee skills and competencies. Thus HRM practice influences management's ability to appropriate the expertise of groups and individuals as an organisational resource.

Resources can thus be viewed as a medium-term product of HRM practices, as they accumulate over a period of time and provide the inputs for the development of long-term capabilities.

Context

HRM practices represent an important influence on the 'inner context' of the organisation (Pettigrew, 1987). The cultural environment of the organisation is not only important in shaping the attitudes and commitments of employees to the sharing of knowledge, but also helps to sustain the shared understandings that allow the circulation of various representations of knowledge, such as specialised language, symbols and stories, throughout the organisation. Indeed, Tyson (1995) highlights the critical role of the HRM practitioner in shaping this emerging 'symbolic order' through which social interactions are interpreted and enacted. In addition, as noted earlier, patterns of 'hard' or 'soft' contracting can have a significant effect on the social capital within an organisation, creating or inhibiting the levels of interpersonal trust which determine the density and richness of social communications.

In these various and often indirect ways, HRM practices help to shape the long-term evolution of organisational capabilities – ie the firm's ability to mobilise its resource base – through the cultivation of human and social capital. The usefulness of differentiating, even in this very abbreviated way, between the impacts and timescales of HRM influences can be summarised as follows.

First, it points us towards the practical points of leverage through which HRM acts upon the management of knowledge, showing the power of such leverage but also the constraints that it may place on short-term initiatives.

Second, as we outline in Figure 4, it also provides us with a way of addressing the interdependency of HRM practices over time – as opposed to the formal interdependency implied by notions of 'internal' and 'external fit'. As we note below, policy influences resources, which in turn influence context, though at each point over a longer time-span and with a more diffuse effect. Subsequently, this inner context influences the range of HRM policy options available to the organisation, and so on.

A third, and for our purposes most important, consequence of unpacking HRM influences in this way is the ability to develop more targeted questions for research – questions that will address some of the specific, practical interactions between HRM and KM. We can readily identify such questions in relation to the different arenas of influence outlined above.

Research questions on the interactions between HRM and KM

Policy questions

◘ What are the effects of aligning HRM policy with KM practices in the context of overall business strategy?

◘ Do the strategies of 'codification' and 'personalisation' provide adequate heuristics for policy alignment, or are other strategic configurations possible?

◘ How are the interrelated configurations of reward systems, development and appraisal, recruitment and selection linked to different forms of KM, and does this vary according to business context?

Resources questions

◘ What are the HRM mechanisms through which individual and group skills may be recognised and appropriated as a resource for the organisation? What is the relative effectiveness of different mechanisms?

◘ Which HRM practices are most effective in recruiting and retaining: (i) expert individuals; or (ii) expert teams, and how does this impact on the organisation's business strategy?

◘ At a strategic level, how do employment patterns – recruitment, retention, career paths – influence the stocks and flows of knowledge in organisations? Are particular forms of knowledge especially vulnerable to employee turnover?

Context questions

◘ What is the effect of different sets of HRM practices on the development of social capital within the organisation? Do patterns of employment security, career development and employee involvement encourage social capital formation – specifically, in relation to levels of trust and the sharing of knowledge?

◘ What are the organisational environments that are most closely associated with the emergence of strong communities of practice? What are the HRM policies and practices that have helped to shape these environments?

◘ What are the implications of measures of human and intellectual capital for the mobilisation of resources? What is the impact on the culture of management and perceptions of knowledge and expertise?

Clearly, the above questions are only a small sub-set of the many different issues that might be relevant to improving our understanding of HRM and KM. However, in seeking to reflect the breadth and richness of what is already known about this critical relationship, we have sought at least to provide some useful insights into the emerging agenda for research – both those areas currently that are under investigation, and, equally importantly, those that are not. It is a commonplace of KM programmes that the most important knowledge in any setting is the knowledge 'we don't know that we don't know'. By comparison, what we do know is only the tip of the iceberg. No doubt, given its limited size and scope, our report has not fully reflected important contributions to this debate. We hope, though, that whatever its positive contribution, it has at least made a negative one by making a small dent in the knowledge 'we don't know' on this topic.

Figure 4 | Interdependency of HRM practices over time

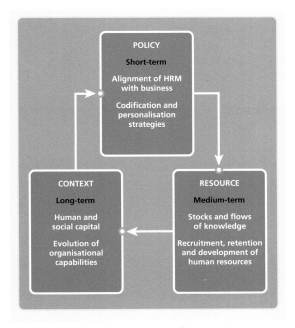

Appendix

Internet resources on knowledge management

Consultancy websites

◪ Arthur Andersen:
http://www.knowledgespace.com/index.htm

◪ Andersen Consulting:
http://www.ac.com/services/knowledge/
km_thought.html

◪ David Skyrme Associates:
http://www.skyrme.com/

◪ Ernst &Young:
http://www.ey.com/knowledge/cbk/default.asp

◪ Erik Sveiby consultancy:
http://www.sveiby.com.au/

Teaching/development resources

◪ Seminar (Maryam Alavi) on KM:
fabweb.is.cityu.edu.hk/isseminar/alavi.htm

◪ Training package – role-play exercise – on
Innovation and the Management of
Knowledge:
http://omni.bus.ed.ac.uk/opsman/oakland/
title.htm

◪ Knowledge World:
http://www.ec2.edu/kworld/

http://www.ec2.edu/dccenter/ok/reports.html

KM technology

◪ Knowledge Management with Intranet
Technology:
http://www.know-net.org/

◪ Open University Knowledge Media Institute:
http://kmi.open.ac.uk/

Information on KM practice

◪ Knowledge online:
http://www.knowledge.org.uk/

◪ The Knowledge Management Forum:
http://www.km-forum.org/

◪ Thomas Davenport's website:
http://www.bus.utexas.edu/kman/

◪ http://www.knowledgemedia.org/
knowledgemedia/knowledgemedia.nsf/pages/
index.html

◪ KM at the American Productivity and
Quality Center:
http://www.apqc.org/topics/topic02.cfm

◪ e-KnowledgeCenter:
http://www.eknowledgecenter.com/

◪ Knowledge Management Network:
http://kmn.cibit.hvu.nl/index.html

◪ Knowledge Inc.:
http://www.knowledgeinc.com/

Discussion groups on KM

◪ http://www.egroups.com/group/knowledge-
management-systems

◪ http://www.brint.com/wwwboard/

Guidelines for KM practice

◪ UMIST KM Audit Tool:
http://nt2.ec.man.ac.uk/usercgi/cric/
cricpaperdl.asp

◘ KPMG's KM assessment framework:
http://kmsurvey.londonweb.net/

Government resources

◘ UK government:
http://www.dti.gov.uk/infoage/index.htm

◘ Australian government:
http://www.isr.gov.au/industry/kbe/

KM consortia

In the wake of the growing interest in KM, a number of multi-organisation consortia have been developed, often with the facilitation of a consultancy organisation, which seek to share best practice across firms.

Centre for the Exploitation of Science and Technology (CEST)

CEST was founded in 1987 as a private–public sector partnership to speed the exploitation of business opportunities. Current membership numbers 35 organisations. CEST has established a Knowledge Management Forum, which is made up of a number of knowledge managers and practitioners from a range of organisations. The forum organises tours of leading KM implementations in the USA and Europe. The website is: http://www.cest.org.uk

European Industrial Management Research Association (EIRMA)

EIRMA brings together technology-based companies with a view to increasing the effectiveness of their industrial innovation and its impact on their business.

The association's comprehensive programme of activities is designed to allow members to exchange views and experience for mutual benefit. Created in 1966 as an independent organisation, EIRMA now involves research managers and scientists from over 170 companies in 21 countries.

EIRMA convenes conferences and produces reports for consortium members and has recently published a report on KM:
http://www.eirma.asso.fr/

Henley Management College Knowledge Management Forum

The Henley Forum brings together business practitioners, industry leaders and experts/academics to help organisations tackle the new challenges presented by the digital information age.

The ongoing programme of workshops, seminars, discussion groups and highly focused research projects spans key issues affecting most functional areas.

http://www.henleymc.ac.uk/HenleyMC.nsf/page/KnowledgeManagement

Institute for Knowledge Management (IKM)

The IKM is a global consortium of member organisations committed to understanding and developing tangible business value from KM. Launched in early 1999 by IBM and Lotus, the IKM conducts action research aimed at advancing the discipline of KM. An international community of over 30 member organisations representing industrial corporations, service firms and government agencies is actively engaged in setting research direction and participating in projects.

IKM's research agenda is based on the conviction that the biggest challenges to deriving value from knowledge management efforts are managerial and social, not technical. Effective knowledge management depends on co-ordinated attention to economic, organisational, cultural and technological issues. This perspective is reflected in research topics such as:

◘ the role of teams and communities in knowledge creation, transfer and reuse

◘ the critical relationship between social capital and knowledge-sharing in organisations

◘ the ways that intermediaries can enable the sharing of expertise

◘ the role of tacit knowledge in the innovative capabilities of firms

◘ the formulation of enterprise-level knowledge strategy.

Contact website: http://ikm.ihost.com/

Magazine articles and interviews

◘ KM:
http://www.kmmagazine.com/

http://62.253.214.142/index.asp

◘ Interview with Peter Drucker:
http://www.wired.com/wired/archive/1.03/drucker.html

◘ Discussion between Drucker and Davenport:
http://www.cio.com/archive/091597_interview_content.html

◘ Knowledge-based organisations:
http://www.forbes.com.forbes/97/0310/5905122a.htm

◘ Knowledge Workers are Different:
http://library.northernlight.com
http://PN20000301030000368.html?cb=13&sc=0#doc

◘ Round table discussion on Knowledge Workers:
http://www.cio.com/archive/050197_round.html

◘ World-Wide Web Virtual Library on Knowledge Management (editor@brint.com):
http://www.brint.com/km/#what

References and bibliography

ABERNATHY W. (1978)

The Productivity Dilemma: Roadblock to innovation in the automobile industry. Baltimore, Johns Hopkins University Press.

ABERNATHY W., CLARK K. AND KANTROW A. (1981)

Industrial Renaissance: Producing a positive future for America. Boston, MIT Press.

ADLER P.S. AND COLE R.E. (1993)

'Designed for learning: a tale of two auto plants'. *Sloan Management Review.* Vol. 34, No. 3. pp85–94.

ALVESSON M. (1993)

'Organization as rhetoric: knowledge-intensive firms and the struggle with ambiguity'. *Journal of Management Studies.* Vol. 30. pp997–1016.

ALVESSON M. (1995)

Management of Knowledge-Intensive Companies. Berlin, Walter de Gruyter.

AMIT R. AND SHOEMAKER P.J.H. (1993)

'Strategic assets and organizational rent'. *Strategic Management Journal.* Vol. 14. pp33–46.

ARGYRIS C. (1992)

On Organizational Learning. Oxford, Blackwell.

BAILYN L. (1988)

'Autonomy in the industrial R&D lab'. In Katz R. (ed.) *Managing Professionals in Innovative Organizations.* New York, Ballinger Publishing Co., pp223–236.

BARNEY J.B. (1991)

'Firm resources and sustained competitive advantage'. *Journal of Management.* Vol. 17, No. 1. pp99–120.

BARRY D. AND ELMES M. (1997)

'Strategy retold: toward a narrative view of strategic discourse'. *Academy of Management Review.* Vol. 22, No. 2. pp429–452.

BAUM J.C. AND INGRAM P. (1997)

'Opportunity and constraint: organizations' learning from the operating and competitive experience of industries'. *Strategic Management Journal.* Vol. 18, Summer Special Issue. pp75–98.

BIJKER W. (1993)

'The social construction of Bakelite: towards a theory of investion'. In Bijker W., Hughes P. and Pinch T. (eds) *The Social Construction of Technological Systems: New directions in the sociology and history of technology.* Cambridge, MA, The MIT Press.

BLACKLER F. (2000A)

Keynote address to the *BPRC 'Knowledge Management: Concepts and Controversies' conference,* Warwick University. 10–11 February.

BLACKLER F. (2000B)

'Knowledge Management'. *People Management.* 21 June.

BOISOT M. (1995)

Information Space. London, Routledge.

BOISOT M. (1998)

Knowledge Assets: Securing competitive advantage in the information economy. Oxford, Oxford University Press.

BONTIS N. (1998)

'Intellectual capital: an exploratory study that develops, measures and models'. *Management Decision.* Vol. 36, No. 2. pp63–76.

BROWN J.S. AND DUGUID P. (1991)

'Organizational learning and communities of practice: toward a unified view of working, learning and innovation'. *Organization Science.* Vol. 2, No. 1. pp40–57.

BROWN J.S. AND DUGUID P. (1998)

'Organizing knowledge'. *California Management Review.* Vol. 40, No. 3. pp90–109.

BURNS T. AND STALKER G. (1961)

The Management of Innovation. London, Tavistock.

CAPELLI P. AND SINGH H. (1992)

'Integrating strategic human resources and strategic management'. In Lewis D., Mitchell O. and Sherer P. (eds) *Research Frontiers in Industrial Relations and Human Resources.* Washington, DC, International Industrial Relations Association.

CHILD J. (1997)

'Strategic choice in the analysis of action, structure, organisations and environment: retrospect and prospect'. *Organisation Studies.* Vol. 18, No. 1. pp43–76.

CHILD J. AND SMITH C. (1987)

'The context and process of organizational transformation'. *Journal of Management Studies.* Vol. 24. pp565–593.

CIBORRA C.U. (1993)

Teams, Markets and Systems: Business innovation and information technology. Cambridge, Cambridge University Press.

CIBORRA C. AND PATRIOTTA G. (1996)

'Groupware and teamwork in new product development: the case of a consumer goods multinational'. In Ciborra C. (ed.) *Groupware and Teamwork*. New York, Wiley.

CLARK P. (1987)

Anglo-American Innovation. Berlin, Du Gruyter.

CLARK P. (2000)

Organisations in Action. London, Routledge.

CLARK P. AND STARKEY K. (1988)

Organisation Transitions and Innovation Design. London, Frances Pinter.

CLARK P. AND STAUNTON N. (1989)

Innovation in Technology and Organisation. London, Routledge.

COLLINS H.M. (1990)

Artificial Experts: Social knowledge and intelligent machines. London, MIT Press.

COLLINSON M., HUTCHINSON S., KINNIE N., PURCELL J., SCARBROUGH H. AND TERRY M. (1998)

'Employment relations in SMEs: customer-driven or market-shaped?' *Employee Relations*. Vol. 21, No. 3. pp218–235.

COLLIS D.J. (1991)

'A resource-based analysis of global competition: a case of the bearings industry'. *Strategic Management Journal*. Vol.13. pp33–48.

CONNER K.R. (1991)

'A historical comparison of resource-based theory and five schools of thought within industrial organisation economics: do we have a new theory of the firm?' *Journal of Management*. Vol. 17. pp121–54.

COOMBS R. AND HULL R. (1998)

'Knowledge management practices and path dependency'. *Research Policy*. Vol. 27. pp237–253.

CUSUMANO M.A. AND SELBY R.W. (1996)

Microsoft Secrets. London, HarperCollins.

DAVENPORT T.H., JARVENPAAA S.L. AND BEERS M.C. (1996)

'Improving knowledge work processes'. *Sloan Management Review*. Summer. pp53–65.

DIERICKX I. AND COOL K. (1989)

'Asset stock accumulation and sustainability of competitive advantage'. *Management Science*. Vol. 35, No. 12. pp1504–1511.

DIXON NANCY M. (1994)

The Organizational Learning Cycle: How we can learn collectively. New York, McGraw-Hill.

DYERSON R. AND MUELLER F. (1999)

'Learning, teamwork and appropriability: managing technological change in the Department of Social Security'. *Journal of Management Studies*. September.

EASTERBY-SMITH M., SNELL R. AND GHERARDI S. (1998)

'Organizational learning: diverging communities of practice'. *Management Learning*. Vol. 29, No. 3. pp259–272.

EASTERBY-SMITH M., BURGOYNE J. AND ARAUJO L (EDS) (1999)

Organizational Learning and the Learning Organization. Thousand Oaks, CA, Sage Publications.

EDVINSSON L. AND MALONE M. (1997)

Intellectual Capital. New York, Harper.

FINCHAM R.J., FLECK R., PROCTER H., SCARBROUGH M., TIERNEY M. AND WILLIAMS R. (1994)

Expertise and Innovation: IT in the financial services sector. Oxford, Clarendon Press.

FOMBRUN C., TICHY N.M. AND DEVANNA M.A. (1984)

Strategic Human Resource Management. Chichester, Wiley.

FRIEDMAN A. WITH CORNFORD D. (1989)

Computer Systems Development: History, organisation and implementation. Chichester, John Wiley & Sons.

GEPPERT M. (1996)

'Paths of managerial learning in the East German context'. *Organization Studies*. Vol. 17, No. 2. pp249–268.

GIBBONS M., LIMOGES C., NOWOTNY H., SCHWARTZMAN S., SCOTT P. AND TROW M. (1994)

The New Production of Knowledge: The dynamics of science and research in contemporary societies. London, Sage.

GINSBERG A. AND ABRAHAMSON E. (1991)

'Champions of change and strategic shifts: the role of internal and external change advocates'. *Journal of Management Studies*. Vol. 28, No. 2. pp173–90.

GORDON C. AND IVES D. (1997)

Knowledge Management Research Study. Toronto, University of Toronto Press.

GRANOVETTER M. (1973)

'The strength of weak ties'. *American Sociological Review.* Vol. 78. pp1360–1380.

GRANOVETTER M. (1985)

'Economic action and social structure: the problem of embeddedness'. *American Journal of Sociology.* Vol. 91, No. 3. pp481–510.

GRANT R.M. (1991)

'The resource-based theory of competitive advantage: implications for strategy formulation'. *California Management Review.* Vol. 33, No. 3, Spring. pp119–135.

GRANT R.M. (1998)

Contemporary Strategy Analysis. 2nd edn. Oxford, Blackwell Publishers.

GUEST D. AND CONWAY N. (1999)

How Dissatisfied are British Workers? A survey of surveys. London, Institute of Personnel and Development.

GUEST D., MICHIE J., SHEEHAN M. AND CONWAY N. (2000)

Employment Relations, HRM and Business Performance. London, Institute of Personnel and Development.

HALL R. (1992)

'The strategic analysis of intangible resources'. *Strategic Management Journal.* Vol. 13. pp135–144.

HAMEL G. AND HEENE A. (EDS) (1994)

Competence-Based Competition. Chichester, Wiley and Sons.

HANSEN G.S. AND WERNERFELT B. (1989)

'Determinants of firm performance: the relative importance of economic and organizational factors'. *Strategic Management Journal.* Vol. 10. pp399–411.

HANSEN M.T. (1999)

'The search transfer problem: the role of weak ties in sharing knowledge across organizational sub-units'. *Administrative Science Quarterly.* Vol. 44. pp82–111.

HANSEN M.T., NOHRIA N. AND TIERNEY T. (1999)

'What's your strategy for managing knowledge?' *Harvard Business Review.* March–April. pp106–116.

HUBER G.P. (1991)

'Organizational learning: the contributing processes and the literature'. *Organization Science.* Vol. 2, No. 1. pp88–115.

KAMOCHE K. (1996)

'Human resource management within a resource-capability view of the firm'. *Journal of Management Studies.* Vol. 33, No. 2. March.

KAMOCHE K. AND MUELLER F. (1998)

'Human resource management and the appropriation-learning perspective'. *Human Relations.* Vol. 51, No. 8. pp1033–1060.

KAPLAN R. AND NORTON D. (1996)

The Balanced Scorecard. Boston, Harvard Business School Press.

KAY J. (1993)

Foundations of Corporate Success. Oxford, Oxford University Press.

KEEGAN A. (1998)

'Management practice in knowledge-intensive firms: the future of HRM in the knowledge era'. Presented at British Academy of Management Conference, Nottingham. September.

KNIGHTS D. AND WILLMOTT H. (EDS) (2000)

The Reengineering Revolution. London, Sage.

KOGUT B. AND ZANDER U. (1992)

'Knowledge of the firm, combinative capabilities and the replication of technology'. *Organization Science.* Vol. 3, No. 3. pp383–397.

KROGH G.V. AND ROOS J. (EDS) (1996)

Managing Knowledge: Perspectives on cooperation and competition. London, Sage.

KUNDA G. (1992)

Engineering Culture: Control and commitment in a high-tech corporation. Philadelphia, Temple University Press.

LADO A.A., BOYD N. AND WRIGHT P. (1992)

'A competency-based model of sustainable competitive advantage: toward a conceptual integration'. *Journal of Management.* Vol. 18, No. 1. pp77–91.

LAVE J. AND WENGER E. (1991)

Situated Learning: Legitimate peripheral participation. Cambridge, Cambridge University Press.

LEWICKI H. J. AND BUNKER B. B. (1996)

'Developing and maintaining trust in work relationship'. In Kramer R. M. and Tyler T. M. (eds) *Trust in Organisations: Frontier of theory and research*. Thousand Oaks, CA, Sage.

LYLES M.A. AND SCHWENK C.R. (1992)

'Top management, strategy and organisational knowledge structures'. *Journal of Management Studies*. Vol. 29, No. 2, March.

LYOTARD J.–L. (1984)

The Post Modern Condition: A report on knowledge. Manchester, Manchester University Press.

MABEY C., SALAMAN G. AND STOREY J. (1998)

Strategic Human Resource Management: A reader. London, Sage.

MACDUFFIE J.P. (1995)

'Human resource bundles and manufacturing performance: organizational logic and flexible production systems in the world auto industry'. *Industrial and Labor Relations Review*. Vol. 48, No. 2. pp197–221.

MAHONEY J.T. AND PANDIAN J. (1992)

'The resource-based view within the conversation of strategic management'. *Strategic Management Journal*. Vol. 13. pp363–380.

MARCH J.G. (1999)

The Pursuit of Organizational Intelligence: Decisions and learning in organizations. Oxford, Blackwell.

MINTZBERG H. (1978)

'Patterns in strategy formation'. *Management Science*. pp934–48.

MINTZBERG H. (1990).

'The design school: reconsidering the basic premises of strategic management'. *Strategic Management Journal*. Vol. 11. pp171–195.

MUELLER F. (1994)

'Teams between hierarchy and commitment: change strategies and the "internal environment"'. *Journal of Management Studies*. Vol. 31, No. 3. pp383–403.

MUELLER F. (1996)

'Human resources as strategic assets: a resource-based evolutionary theory'. *Journal of Management Studies*. Vol. 33, No. 6, November. pp757–85.

NAHAPIET J. AND GHOSHAL S. (1998)

'Social capital, intellectual capital and the organizational advantage'. *Academy of Management Review*. Vol. 23, No. 2. pp242–266.

NONAKA I. (1991)

'The knowledge-creating company'. *Harvard Business Review*. November–December. pp96–104.

NONAKA I. AND TAKEUCHI H. (1995)

The Knowledge Creating Company. New York, Oxford University Press.

ORR J.E. (1990)

'Sharing knowledge, celebrating identity: community memory in a service culture'. In Middleton D. and Edwards D. (eds) *Collective remembering*. London, Sage, pp169–189.

PAN S.L. AND SCARBROUGH H. (1998)

'A socio-technical view of knowledge sharing at Buckman Laboratories'. *Journal of Knowledge Management*. Vol. 2, No.1. pp55–66.

PATTERSON M., WEST M., LAWTHOM R. AND NICKELL S. (1997)

Impact of People Management Practices on Business Performance. London, Institute of Personnel and Development.

PEDLER M., BURGOYNE J. AND BOYDELL T. (1991)

The Learning Company: A strategy for sustainable development. London, McGraw-Hill.

PETERAF M.A. (1993)

'The cornerstones of competitive advantage: a resource-based view'. *Strategic Management Journal*. Vol. 14. pp179–191.

PETERS T. AND WATERMAN R.H. (1982)

In Search of Excellence. New York, Random House.

PETRASH G. (1996)

'Dow's journey to a knowledge value management culture'. *European Management Journal*. Vol. 14, No. 4. pp365–374.

PETTIGREW A.M. (1987)

'Context and action in the transformation of the firm'. *Journal of Management Studies*. Vol. 24, No. 6. pp649–670.

POLANYI M. (1962)

Personal Knowledge: Towards a post-critical philosophy. New York, Harper.

PORTER M.E. (1980)

Competitive Strategy. New York, Free Press.

PORTER M.E. (1991)

'Towards a dynamic theory of strategy'. *Strategic Management Journal.* Vol. 12. pp95–117.

POWELL W., KOPUT K. AND SMITH-DOERR L. (1996)

'Interorganizational collaboration and the locus of innovation: networks of learning in biotechnology'. *Administrative Science Quarterly.* Vol. 41. pp116–145.

PRAHALAD C.K. AND HAMEL G. (1990)

'The core competence of the corporation'. *Harvard Business Review.* May–June. pp79–91.

PRICHARD C., HULL R., CHUMER H. AND WILLMOTT H. (EDS) (2000)

Managing Knowledge: Critical investigations of work and learning. London, Macmillan.

PRUSAK L. (1997)

Knowledge in Organizations. Oxford, Butterworth-Heinemann.

QUINN J. (1980)

Strategies for Change: Logical incrementalism. Homewood, IL, Irwin.

QUINN J.B., ANDERSON P. AND FINKELSTEIN S. (1996)

'Managing professional intellect: making the most of the best'. *Harvard Business Review.* Vol. 74, March–April. pp71–80.

RAJAN A., LANK E. AND CHAPPLE K. (1998)

Good Practices in Knowledge Creation and Exchange. Tunbridge Wells, Create.

REICH R. (1991)

The Wealth of Nations: Preparing ourselves for 21st century capitalism. London, Simon & Schuster.

RICHARDSON R. AND THOMPSON M. (1999)

The Impact of People Management Practices on Business Performance: A literature review. London, Institute of Personnel and Development.

ROOS JN, ROOS G. AND DRAGONETTI N. (1998)

Intellectual Capital: Navigating in the new business landscape. New York, New York University Press.

RUGGLES R. (1998)

'The state of the notion: knowledge management in practice'. *California Management Review.* Vol. 40, No. 3. pp80–89.

RUMELT R P., SCHENDEL D. AND TEECE D.J. (1991)

'Strategic management and economics'. *Strategic Management Journal*, Special Issue: Fundamental Research Issues in Strategy and Economics. Vol. 12.

SANCHEZ R. AND HEENE A. (EDS) (1997)

Strategic Learning and Knowledge Management. New York, John Wiley.

SCARBROUGH H. (1995)

'Blackboxes, hostages and prisoners'. *Organization Studies.* Vol. 16. pp991–1020.

SCARBROUGH H. (1999)

'Knowledge as work: a conflict-based analysis of the management of knowledge workers'. *Technology Analysis and Strategic Management.* Vol. 11, No. 1. pp5–16.

SCARBROUGH H. (2000)

'HR implications of supply chain relationships'. *Human Resource Management Journal.* Vol. 10, No. 1. pp5–17.

SCARBROUGH H. AND BURRELL G. (1996)

'The axeman cometh: the changing roles and knowledges of middle managers'. In Clegg S. and Palmer G. (eds) *The Politics of Management Knowledge.* London, Sage.

SCARBROUGH H. AND SWAN J. (1999)

Case Studies in Knowledge Management. London, Institute of Personnel and Development.

SCARBROUGH H., SWAN J. AND PRESTON J. (1999)

Knowledge Management: A literature review. London, Institute of Personnel and Development.

SENGE P. (1990)

The Fifth Discipline: The art and practice of the learning organisation. London, Doubleday.

SHOEMAKER P.J.H. (1993)

'Strategic decisions in organisations: rational and behavioural views'. *Journal of Management Studies.* Vol. 30, No. 1. pp107–129.

SHRIVASTAVA P. (1985)

'Integrating strategy formulation with organizational culture'. *The Journal of Business Strategy.* Vol. 5, No. 3, Winter. pp103–111.

SIMON H.A. (1991)

'Bounded rationality and organizational learning'. *Organization Science.* Vol. 2, No. 1.

SPENDER J.C. (1989)

Industry Recipes. Oxford, Blackwell.

SPENDER J.C. (1996)

'Organizational knowledge, learning and memory: three concepts in search of a theory'. *Journal of Organizational Change Management.* Vol. 9. pp63–78.

STALK G., EVANS P. AND SHULMAN L.E. (1992)

' Competing on capabilities: the new rules of corporate strategy'. *Harvard Business Review.* Vol. 92. pp57–69.

STARBUCK W.H. (1992)

'Learning by knowledge intensive firms'. *Journal of Management Studies.* Vol. 29, No. 6, November. pp713–740.

STERN E. AND SOMMERLAD E. (1999)

Workplace Learning, Culture and Performance. London, Institute of Personnel and Development.

STEWART T. (1997)

Intellectual Capital: The new wealth of organizations. New York, Doubleday.

STOREY J. (ED.) (1989)

New Perspectives on Human Resource Management. London, Routledge.

SULLIVAN P.H. (ED.) (1998)

Profiting from Intellectual Capital. New York, John Wiley.

SVEIBY K. (1997)

The New Organizational Wealth: Managing and measuring knowledge-based assets. San Francisco, Berrett-Koehler.

SWAN J. (1999)

Knowledge Management and the People Management Gap. Presentation given to the BPRC, June.

TAMPOE M. (1993)

'Motivating knowledge workers: The challenge for the 1990s'. *Long Range Planning.* Vol. 26.

TEECE D. (1998)

'Capturing value from knowledge assets: the new economy, markets for know-how and intangible assets'. *California Management Review.* Vol. 40, No. 3. pp55–79.

TSOUKAS H. (1996)

'The firm as a distributed knowledge system: a constructionist approach'. *Strategic Management Journal.* Vol. 17, Special Issue. pp11–25.

TYSON S. (1995)

Human Resource Strategy: Towards a general theory of HRM. London, Pitman.

TYSON S. AND FELL A. (1986)

Evaluating the Personnel Function. London, Hutchinson.

WERNERFELT B. (1984)

'A resource-based view of the firm'. *Strategic Management Journal.* Vol. 5. pp171–180.

WERNERFELT B. (1989)

'From critical resources to corporate strategy'. *Journal of General Management.* Vol. 14, No. 3. pp4–12.

WHALLEY P. AND ORR J.E. (1997)

'Technical work in the division of labour'. In Barley S.R. and Orr J.E. (eds) *Between Craft and Science: Technical work in US settings.* London, ILR Press.

WHIPP R. AND CLARK P. (1986)

Innovation and the Auto Industry. London, Frances Pinter.

WHITTINGTON R. (1988)

'Environmental structure and theories of strategic choice'. *Journal of Management Studies.* Vol. 25, No. 6. pp521–536.

WHITTINGTON R. (1993)

What is Strategy and Does it Matter? London, Routledge.

WILKINSON A. AND WILLMOTT H. (1995)

Making Quality Critical. London, Routledge.

WINTER S. (1987)

'Knowledge and competence as strategic assets'. In Teece D.J. (ed.) *The Competitive Challenge: Strategies for industrial innovation and renewal.* Cambridge, MA, Ballinger Publishing Co., pp159–184.

WOOD S. (1995)

'The four pillars of HRM: are they connected?' *Human Resource Management Journal.* Vol. 5, No. 5. pp48–58.